Pathways

humanity's search for its soul

ISBN: 1093487356

ISBN-13: 978-1093487350

Pathways

humanity's search for its soul

Simon Cole

Other books by the same author:

Along the Way :
themed meditations for day to day living
Amazon 2016

Stillness in Mind :
a companion to mindfulness, meditation and
living
Changemakers Books 2014

Being Still, Being Now :
a companion to mindfulness
Amazon 2013

CONTENTS

FOREWORD

This is not a book for those in a hurry. It will not satisfy readers who look for clear and cogently argued answers to the existential questions that seem ever more urgently to confront humanity as we hurtle towards ecological, social and political disaster.

Simon Cole's purpose in these pages lies in an altogether different dimension. Like all spiritual and mystical writers who have served an arduous apprenticeship, he is concerned not with solving problems but with changing attitudes and with altering perceptions. The world which he inhabits is not the domain of black and white, of either/or, of for or against. He invites us instead into the altogether more demanding world of paradox, uncertainty, timelessness and the greater context beyond the human. Above all he confronts us with the challenge of true encounter and, inspired by the work and example of Martin Buber, we discover what it might mean to be fully interdependent and committed to real connectedness at a time when we seem to be communicating frenetically in every possible technological mode and becoming increasingly alienated from each other and from the planet on which we depend.

Simon Cole writes beautifully and his book is itself a kind of lyrical meditation while being the fruit of many years' experience as a therapist and spiritual explorer. What is more, it bears the marks of a deep humility which encourages confidence in his reader and makes the savouring of his words an experience which stills the mind and nourishes the soul.

BRIAN THORNE
Emeritus Professor of Counselling, University of East Anglia
Lay Canon, Norwich Cathedral

"Meeting is not in space and time, but space and time in meeting."

Martin Buber

Whisperings

Throughout its existence humankind has created pathways… where one has gone and found a way, then been followed by another, so the way becomes a path. A way needs a following to become a path and the path needs to offer an arrival to become the way (for few paths end nowhere and even those that do marked someone's arrival once). The path which disappears in the distance has been a marker for so many lives and been confirmed by them with their passing - so many stories preserved in the clay by so many feet, hope kindled along its winding course.

This book is about pathways - pathways on the ground, pathways in the mind, pathways of illusion and allusion, pathways which are ours and pathways which we share. Perhaps it will seem a spiritual book, of itself a meditation, but it is not in any sense a religious book, though I make reference to 'religion'. How to make that distinction? It is probably easiest to say that religions have their tenets of faith and their rituals, to confirm and deepen that faith amongst their followers. In this way even the more loosely organised and minimally doctrinal religions offer a comforting sense of belonging via a shared perspective.

The spiritual, on the other hand, does not have any shared object. And so, my spirituality is mine alone and yours is yours. They may - indeed they must - show themselves differently in each of us, and, though it might feel like they share a similar plane of our being, each is individual, and inalienably part of the unique person we each are. Which means of course that there can be no sense of belonging, in the way that a shared faith, as religion, creates a belonging, unless, that is, we look to our being human as the way we create our sense of feeling a part of something. So, in terms of the spiritual, the question predicated here is not "Of what religion or faith are you?" and it is not even "Are you a spiritual person?"; rather it is "*How* are you *your own* spiritual person?" And in the end, perhaps, how may we each find the essence of a shared spiritual growth which has the power to transform and hopefully rescue our human species on the earth.

My premise, then, is not so much, "there is a spiritual side in everyone", a consciousness of the non-material waiting to be awakened in each of us, but that our spirituality is unerringly manifest already and that the limitation is in the looking, not in the deficiency. To see it is to create it. So further, what is asked of us is to bring into a shared and collective consciousness, that which is already in existence, though often dimly perceived.

Readers of "Stillness in Mind"[1] will know that my own philosophy of life and living rests firmly on the insights of Martin Buber, who, whilst being an Hasidic Jew with the unique spirituality that this imbued in him, also drew inspiration from Søren Kierkegaard, a linking in spirit

---

[1] "Stillness in Mind: a companion to mindfulness, meditation and living",
Changemakers Books, Winchester & New York, 2014

which transcended the boundaries of their individual faiths.

In "Stillness in Mind" I sought to offer a means to be with oneself in an accepting and empathic way, using self-awareness as a regenerative process - an inner, though not inward-looking, experience. Here, I am concerned with the significance of being our own conscious and spiritual person with a shared and collective awareness. My perspective is not political, though if you put 'person' and 'collective' together in the same sentence it is difficult to avoid that aspect. But I would rather it be a view of the particular in the global and the global in the particular. With Buber I want to say "All real living is meeting" and discover the scope for true meeting and genuine dialogue in our inter-connecting world, discover humanity's soul.

But the sensing of a political dimension is inevitable, and will show itself here, as questions inevitably start to arise for the reader too...

> *"Relative to our own lifespan we've been around quite a long time, us humans, and we've got all these ideas about living together, how come we're not doing a better job by now?"*

> *"If we'd only learnt a better way to do things - more jaw less war - how many more decisions and discoveries might there have been, which could have meant that our survival today was less precarious?"*

> *"By now you'd think there was something we could have learnt, some insight about getting on together, which would release us from the endless round of conflict?... just to be able to lead fulfilling lives without it being at someone else's expense!"*

These are philosophical rather than overtly political questions. Nonetheless, if they are the sort of questions which have floated into your mind in your more reflective moments, then come on this journey now, a journey along pathways which might lead to freedom, the kind of freedom which is not a rose garden and certainly not *Nirvana*, but a kind of freedom nonetheless, a freedom which at its heart is an attitude of mind.

A little like physicists who have for years been searching for the algorithm which lies at the origin of the universe and might explain matter in all its many forms, my work in psychological therapy over many years has led me to wonder about the essential nature of existence as a human being, which is manifest in what we each know as our encounter with life... and other people! From time to time for me there has been a glimpse, a charge of energy suggesting an elemental connectedness in all experience, that cardinal simplicity, before it is too quickly overlaid with concepts and perspectives and formulations...

> *through a break in the cloud an unexpected shaft of sunlight suddenly illuminating an indistinct detail in the landscape, but also casting into shadow the far side of a rocky outcrop on the mountain; a sudden breeze disturbing the leaves in the trees, revealing darting shots of bright colour, a glimpse of richness glinting somewhere behind, beyond, but then hidden again.*

It can seem as if that simplest primary core, the first line of the code, itself has a guile like that of a master player using a smokescreen to cloak his strategy.

Or perhaps we are the smokescreen.

Yet some have come closer to finding our soul.

Buber, whom some believe the only true philosopher of the twentieth century (where others like Husserl, Freud, Sartre, were only [sic] thinkers), saw that our *manner* of being conscious lies at the root of the world we each know as reality; that we have the option to perform alone in a play in which there are no other parts, or engage in a drama of living where the script is written in the moment of each encounter. To engage we must meet and that meeting cannot be a face-off along a rigidly held line of demarcation: real meeting brings the uncertainties of contact and the challenges of participation. Reading Buber, more than anything we have the sense of being at the very start of that process of discovery which is Man's encounter with living, his discovery of himself and his fellow-creatures through consciousness.

To live we must encounter others and it is this encounter which offers to humankind, as individuals, as societies, as nations, as populations, even as a species alongside other species on a shared planet, the opportunity of affirmation or the misery of desolation. At all levels and in all aspects of living we can choose to meet, with a wishing to give and a willingness to receive (because both are needed), and engage with mutuality and reciprocity. Or we can cast the other, be they human, animal or the whole of nature, collectively or individually, as our domain for control and manipulation.

Encounter, though, has a more fundamental implication still, for the primary encounter is with ourselves. We did not choose it, we inherited it, and it is what we are: conscious – self-conscious – animals. There are those wonderful lines of Rilke, which so poignantly encapsulate this aspect of the human condition:

We know what is really out there only from
the animal's gaze; for we take the very young
child and force it around, so that it sees
objects – not the Open, which is so
deep in animals' faces. Free from death.
We, only, can see death; the free animal
has its decline in back of it forever,
and God in front, and when it moves, it moves
already in eternity...
And where we see the future, it sees all time
and itself within all time, forever healed.[2]

The fundamental process of nature, that of life sustaining life in a self-perpetuating flow of compensating adjustment, reviving declining evolving, was broken with us. Was broken by us. Consciousness was a shift without a counterpoint.

With consciousness comes differentiation and the inevitability of comparison, not just comparison of ourself with another, but comparison of the possibilities of many a hypothetical self, and so of many other presents. Possibility, though, has a flip-side: openings and beginnings create closings and endings, and so our consciousness deprives us of living in eternity and substitutes the torment of mortality. Along with mortality we inherit anxiety and self-doubt, impatience and frustration, sadness and resignation. But it is granted also that we know - connection and community, fulfilment and harmony, belief and consummation. The former trap us in the cell of a solitary confinement. But with the latter we are on the highway of relation, the essence of our being as a

---

[2] From Eighth Elegy by Rainer Maria Rilke; this translation by Stephen Miller

conscious species played out through our struggle with knowing ourselves in the company of others. It is this struggle which is the source of all achievements of our humankind and manifests in societies, customs, institutions, individuals, peoples... the stories of our passage on the planet. These are the pathways. Pathways of living, pathways of seeking understanding, pathways of healing.

The human animal is trapped in its actualising impulse of expansion and exploitation, the inexorable conclusion to which might only be self-destruction, but humanity's flowering amidst a vast and indifferent universe will have been an ennobling (and, just possibly, enduring) phenomenon, for all its minuscule impact outside its own meagre sphere.

This work is a recognition of that flowering of the species that knew itself, could do ill and could do well, could wound itself and could restore itself, but could never change its fundamental nature. Arrogant and humble, powerful and powerless, it would always be searching for the healing pathway, the pathway to a kind of freedom.

Setting Out

If we ask ourselves how much of the time we are really connecting with the world around, we are likely to be confronted by the uncomfortable observation that it is really not very much. Of course that does not mean we do not talk to people - we probably do, a lot - on the phone, through social media, by texting, with email and all the plethora of ways which modern technology provides for us to be up to date. We pass on information. Information flow is of the essence of modern society and we have become very good at it. But we've done more than that – uncomfortable with the notion of 'information' being rather stark, we have tried to humanise it (in the interests of reassuring ourselves) by designating it as 'communication'. Communication has a positive spin because it infers that it is for someone else's benefit, not just our own. "I communicate in order to be of help to you." Or rather, "I communicate because I want you to know that I am being helpful to you." Or again, "I communicate because I want to feel good about myself that I am being helpful to you." Or more dis-engaging than any of these, "I communicate in order that you cannot say I haven't told you."

But all this communication is not connection.

Too often the domain of communication, on an individual level, is a world of our own making, a world we have constructed to fit in with how we see ourselves, a world we fashion to minimise its dissonance with our self-image. So… if we are feeling good about ourselves, to be turned down when we offer to lend a hand to a friend who is struggling to keep up, for instance, will have little effect. And if we have a down on ourselves, a colleague who has no time to explain something we don't understand will be heard as confirming that we are not important enough to be worthy of concern. This world we construct, whether it's our mood of the moment or something more enduring affecting our self-esteem, is something we apply to whatever is around: we read into any answer what we want to hear. Which means that most communication is essentially one way and any response (if we even give room for a response, that is) is interpreted according to our expectation of what it 'should' be, in other words, what we can allow it to be.

Communication, as we practise it in the everyday, has many forms and many purposes, but genuinely connecting is rarely one of them. We maintain a safe distance so that we are not really putting ourselves at risk - "so long as I keep talking, they can't put me on the spot". Safer this way by far, because true connectedness demands immediacy and is unpredictable. Connection can never be a one way process - to connect we must give but we must also receive. No matter whether the response from the other side is verbalised or not, for a true connection to be made I must receive (take in) what comes. And then I have to accept the possibility that I will be affected, though I cannot know how: I cannot forearm myself for what comes back. All is not lost though: the old adage "sticks and stones can break your bones but words can hurt you never" is pertinent because in the end we can mediate our emotional response to a verbal attack, we can be responsible for how we feel (to use a rather hackneyed counselling line), and the more so if we have an understanding of how this whole field of communication and connection works.

Then we can go further than being connected. We can engage. Engagement demands yet more from us. It draws on will and intention. It requires our interest, not just in maintaining a reciprocating *process* of giving and receiving, but in the *content* of what is given and received and how it develops. We could call it a form of commitment - not to an outcome necessarily, but to participation in a journey.

In many ways it might feel as if the cart was coming before the horse, were we to talk about commitment before thinking about commitment to what. But in the same way that so many conflicts, rebellions and insurrections of the later twentieth and early twenty-first centuries have shown that resolution cannot come from force of arms, but only through political means, commitment and engagement show themselves to be the only means by which communication becomes the channel for the humanising of humankind. Even if it is no more than a commitment to continue our engagement, it is a step we can always take for our betterment, as individuals, as societies, as nations, ultimately as co-occupiers of this planet.

And so the meeting becomes the pathway.

We cannot engage without meeting. And we cannot journey without a path. They are necessary conditions. Together they can become the way.

From the Beginning

When was the last time you listened to the silence?

In the beginning, the very beginning, there was silence.

The 'Big Bang', despite its name, could not have been heard by anyone even if there had been anyone to hear. It was energy expanding and until the temperature started to fall and the basic elements of matter condense, there could be no sound. Our universe began without a fanfare.

In the vacuum of space there is no sound.

But we do not live in that space, limitless space. We live in 'our' space, which is always circumscribed by the limits that our awareness in each moment is applying. Our attention in any moment may be spatial or it may be relational or it may be cerebral, but it is always bounded with a cordon which we cannot break through. And in our space, this space, there is never silence. There cannot be.

We have *never* been able to listen to the silence.

Even in *our* beginning, our own individual beginning, there was not silence. The womb was a noisy place. Yet, paradoxically, in those times when we go behind the interference - peripheral sounds, thought chatter, physical tension - to describe the soundless space we reach out to, we use words that echo our romantic womb-image... wrapt, surrounded, immersed, blanket. As if there is a comfort in the notion of somewhere away from the clamour, albeit we are reaching beyond our remembered experience.

In a world of tumult and turmoil, the associations we make with silence resonate with our most deeply-felt yearnings: peace, stillness, tranquillity. Such comfort we seek to discover through solitude, withdrawal, retreat.

What is it about us, social animal that we are, that at times we demand the isolation of our very being in the containment of our own self-awareness, seeking to set that in a context of infinity, the endlessness of space, the nothingness of silence? It feels like the response to a tension vaguely sensed between a 'now' which is immediate and apparent and manifest, and an 'ever' which is felt as a compulsion for a place in the passage of creation - our place in eternity, to lend meaning to a life, a purpose even, and confirm that our existence need not always be circumscribed by relativity.

In a monastery on Mount Athos, a rocky promontory high above Homer's "wine-dark" sea, a father Seraphim will talk to you about meditation and he will start with this sense of the eternal. In his tradition of hesychasm, a practise in the Eastern Orthodox churches, the practitioner retires inward, sublimating even their senses to make contact with the eternal in God. The origin of the name of this pathway of meditation comes from ancient Greek words meaning stillness, rest, silence, words that foster the idea of inner being. But the father Seraphim will point to the mountain and exhort you to contemplate its outward presence and sit in meditation in *its* way. In our time-span the mountain is unmoving, anchored at our point in the flow of creation. But our view is relative and the mountain *is* moving, moving and changing, from a time immemorial before our species began to a time invisible beyond our extinction. In watching the mountain, he will tell you, you can feel the transience of your being in the ongoing narrative of creation, released from the dominion of self. The mountain is simply there. And its presence silent.

Since the time when man's growing mastery of his immediate material circumstances allowed the occasional break for reflection and simply gazing out, right through to our present day, humans have stared at mountains. What do we see? A world removed? A world contained? A world complete? A presence beyond our own? Unapproachable proximity[3]? Above all perhaps they invoke mystery with their sense of not needing us: where *we* are needy of everything we gather around us in our own world, the mountain just is, in the way that we ourselves so often yearn to be able to just be. It stirs in us that illusion that we would find peace in its containment; we anticipate joy from a kind of holding, like a child skipping behind the Pied Piper. But the support that the mountain offers is of a different kind. It is a linking with our eternity - at once cold, impersonal, silent, but also connecting, affirming, grounding - when, with the hesychast on Mount Athos, we find the path to the strength

---

[3] 'une inapprochable proximité' is an expression used by Jean-Yves Leloup in "Manque et Plénitude" (*"Poverty and Plenty"*)

within ourselves, as we sit alongside the vast presence of the massif.

In meditation, though, that path within is not bound to be comfortable. Before the stillness of pure contact with a divine comes the arena in which the spirits of the ego work their disruptive manoeuvres. Often impatient of the slow persistent work of meditation and self-understanding, but craving release from our self-inflicted struggle, in most cultures we have projected our source of salvation beyond and above. That source of deliverance - whether punishment or absolution - we have expected to come from on high, from the mountain. For the ancient Greeks the gods resided on Olympus from where they dispensed justice to humans for their hubris, the extreme version of which is the belief that "I" am right because I am "me". Overweening pride. The ego supreme. For the Israelites after the exodus, Mount Sinaï was where Moses received their God's conditions. Mount Kailas in Tibet is the home of Shiva, one of the 'Great Gods' of Hinduism. The same mountain is home to Samvara, a representation of the Buddha and, earlier still, the sacred origin of the Bon religion. While for Christians "heaven" cannot escape being associated with somewhere away from earth, which, inevitably, means the sky, a location 'corroborated' by descriptions of events such as the Ascension.

The notion of something beyond reach, physically and intellectually, has always served as the vehicle for our projections, but faith, if it is the sentiment we need to maintain the illusion of integrity, veils rather than resolves, the inner conflict. Each painstaking step mankind has taken along the evolving course of social, artistic and intellectual development that we call civilisation, creating myths around succeeding stages accomplished on the epic journey, acquiring faiths as talismans for immortality, each painstaking step seems to beg the question - "What would it take to be satisfied?" The response comes back "To not be human, to be immortal" and mirrors the tension between the tumult of living and the silence of creation. The elephant in the room is our own myopia - if only we could touch on the silence which lies beneath the tumult, then the pain of growing up and the wounds from lessons not learnt would be healed... if only mankind could connect with the silence of the spheres, he would discover the balm of true peace. Yet for all of us it is possible to sit and slowly allow a stillness to come over us, not willing anything, but simply allowing our bodies to become all that they are, our breathing the only token of our presence in the world. Seeking nothing, we would simply be. Like the still point at the axis of the turning world, where motion is motionless and silence is a void.

~ ~ ~

In a small village close to the dunes on the northern edge of the Sahara, where hard-baked dirt roads are whisked by sand and where buildings have the same grey unadorned mud-brick lines they have had for millenia, where the mosque walls support a lean-to general store, there is a sense of hanging in time. You may see a solitary figure in a djellaba - it is winter now, so the temperature only reaches the low thirties centigrade - walking staunchly down the road; occasionally there will be Berber wives sitting outside their houses shielding their faces from your intrusion, most likely children scattered in empty spaces - boys, no girls - but nothing to dispel the void of time hanging.

Sitting as the sun goes down, looking out toward the

palm trees which separate the village from the dunes, listening to young voices conversing across the rooftops, you start to understand the nature of stillness. The ethereal chatter marks out the silence, which lies like a blanket on the dusty desert earth; sounds creating, not breaking, the quiet; a deep calm untouched in the static air.

Walk out of the village towards the dunes and first you pass through the belt of vegetation - this is an oasis, after all - where each village household has a meagre cultivable strip, irrigated through narrow channels where the spring water is switched daily to give each plot its turn. In this world there are three colours - the blue of the sky, the light orange Sahara sand and the vivid green of living plants and palms. When you have passed through this haven of moisture and shade, there will be only two.

Leaving, you must climb, because the dunes are hills, some are hundreds of feet high, and they are moving; with a vapour of sand particles blurring each crest, they slowly transform and imperceptibly shift their great bulk to the tune of an orchestrating wind. Reaching a crest you see another and another, an endless labyrinth of sinuous undulating emptiness.

A palette now of blue and dusty orange. The world suddenly simplified. Wind, sand, sun. And whatever you are bringing.

As if the simplicity of the stark surroundings and the searchlight beam of a scorching sun would lay bare the human soul in its minimal significance for the planet and its inadequacy in the face of a perfect godhead, we have always come to the desert to discover ourselves; to the place where no external variation can distract. Within a couple of centuries of the death of Christ, the Desert

Fathers, coptic monks from Alexandria, were living in the Egyptian desert. The inspiration for the brothers on Mount Athos and the Benedictine order, they attracted others, and soon there were over a thousand, hermit monks, ascetics, small communities, and with them the tradition of hesychasm came into being - a silence within for continual prayer.

For the Desert Fathers, the call was to a self-renunciation in the face of their absolute belief in the necessity of a devotee's faith. For others down the centuries who have followed their footsteps, without a faith but still a kind of fervour, it has been a search for clarity through understanding. Pare down your world to its barest skeleton. Ego exposed. And neutralised. Earth's desert for a desert of the soul. Now, surely, there will be an answer... in the wind, in the heat and the cold, in the two searing primary colours, in the emptiness. But the desert is only a discipline. The answer always comes from within.

The process can work, though: the minimal, wherever it might be manifest, as the counterpoint for our being. Not so much a method of exposing the soul, as of holding a gaze. At one end of the spectrum the gaze may be held through solitude in the desert, this commitment to an unspecified period in a brutally harsh environment, but at the other by intentional and disciplined practice, within the humdrum of an ordinary life, through a looking within using meditation. The metaphor of the soul encompassed with emptiness applies to both. The discoveries with each come from replacing our human urge to always 'be at something' and always stepping forward to be somewhere else, with an abiding with what is and a persistence in just being here where we are. Eugene Gendlin[4] offered a route for discovering our most meaningful process in the moment, touching that edge of awareness which is sensed rather than articulated in thought or identified as a feeling. At our edge of awareness we can locate something else - something we know that we know, but for which our cognitive mind has not yet completed the links. The sensing is almost visceral, like leaning over an edge to the point where gravity is about to take over, and then it does, and you realise you are flying. Look down now and you can see the terrain, which your fear of falling no longer obscures. The terrain 'makes sense': it has a logic and consistency which we can see, now that the blockage has been removed and a link made.

There is a route we can take in meditation to open up a pathway for understanding. It is the route we find we are following in the desert, each footfall on a surface which keeps no record, in a landscape which does not even acknowledge our existence. No track to follow, no trace left. The ultimate clear space. Stand now in the broad deep bowl between these shifting hills of sand, unyielding underfoot, here and there textures of rock superficially whitened, sandy swirls drifting on hardened ripples of a prehistoric sea like the ephemeral brushing of awareness forming. Start up a dune, sinking in the soft sand, straining muscle-paining effort, then the sand hardening on its flank, crisped by the wind-shadow on freezing nights, but still a steepening aching slope to the soft sharp ridge. Sit astride the sand-whale and gaze out over an

---

[4] Gendlin was the originator of the Focusing method, a way of achieving change steps in one's personal life, which became an international movement in the seventies to the present day. He was a colleague of Carl Rogers at Chicago University.

endless landscape unaltered by human hand, undifferentiated by nature's intervention.

When we look within it is hard to find the clarity of an unobscured view. Layers of 'noise' come between and clutter up our gaze. Surface noise, the twittering chatter of daily irritants - the "why can't?" "not again" "she could" "that's me" "not now" "give up" - incessant babble of uncompleted work and re-work. Below this surface, the slower swell of unfulfilled intention and desire, a landscape forming and re-forming, fault lines present, sometimes clear, sometimes hidden, and always with potential to reveal themselves and mar the outlook or change the course. But if we are patient and allow the surface rippling to be still and the swell subside, we can hear the beat of our being behind our breathing, the rhythm of the earth itself. This is the desert floor.

~ ~ ~

Vermilion is the colour of the sunset in the desert, the burning disc igniting, drawing down its captured world, dunes now dark orange slowly becoming black until the switch is flicked, the light is gone and scorching sand turns cold. Sit still and wait. Your eyes must cease their recoil from the glaring brightness of the day. Here is a different world. Here you can only feel your way, follow a direction through the chaos of dunes until exhausted, washed up on an endless shore, you stretch out on a bed made hard by the chilly touch of night. The passing of the day has opened up a space so vast the mind shivers. You are adrift in a gleaming sky of a trillion stars. Sleeping in a soundless eternity.

Briefly before dawn comes a chill breeze from the east, and you shiver in the disappearing night. Look out over a day's journey-worth of flat harsh stoney plain to the mountains beyond, picked out against a sky very slowly turning pink. The breeze stilling now, leaving only a sense of something coming closer... no sound, no movement... then, a light-speed arrow of burnished gold shoots across the plain and strikes the dunes - shapes suddenly given form, grey melting to orange and red, a blinding disc burning away the horizon, the sun, the sun is back.

And still no sound.

You will never come closer to the silence at the birth of the universe.

~ ~ ~

We could say that we only know that we exist in terms of what is happening to us and that there are two primary features of our awareness of our existence, namely, our world changing around us and our mind interpreting this. Our attention is grabbed by something changing and simultaneously we interpret what has changed and its significance for us. The process of interpreting has many tiers, but first there is the stimulus of the change, which causes our noticing. The stimulus being noticed indicates awareness and awareness signifies a 'joining'. It is the joining which is the first indicator of existence. Awareness is firstly this joining, brought into existence by a change. After that may come a description, a contextualisation, an understanding, but these are all different levels of interpretation, building on the awareness. Before them has come the joining, as the token of existence. And existence, in the joining, is the ending of nothing.

Sound, but more specifically music, is unique in its way of creating a channel between nothing and existence. Music could be as old as language: flutes made out of bones have been discovered, which are 40,000 years old. Superficially music serves no function in nourishing or protecting us, but over the last twenty years it has been discovered that it prompts activity across wide areas of the brain, even in memory and reasoning functions. In terms of our sense of our being, music holds us at the level of pure awareness: further interpretation is foiled because all music is abstract[5]. Whereas a sound which is not a musical sound will have us wondering about its source and the nature of what is creating it, a first note of music may have us asking what instrument is playing it, but with far less mental activity and far less insistence. And more than this, music draws us in, calling up appreciation and expectation. It always evokes a response from us.

In this way it also initiates an *ongoing* flow of awareness, because our response does not end when the note can no longer be heard, even if no other notes follow. If you are able, take a stringed instrument - violin, guitar or piano - sit quietly for a few moments and then play just one note, somewhere in the octave above or below middle C. (If you are using a violin do not use the bow, just pluck the string, if you are using a piano, press the key and hold it down.) Listen to the note you have played. Listen by letting the note be all that is happening for you, 'look' at the note, letting it fill your being and move in your consciousness. Listen until you can no longer hear the sound and then go on listening in the space which it has left... the space will

---

[5] The designation of certain genre as "programme music" does not contradict this: our understanding of particular music as having a story comes later in the sequence of interpretation, later relatively than understanding the meaning of a word. The same could be said of singing: the note comes before the end of the first word.

be 'coloured' by where the note has carried you.[6]

But music in its essence is note *and* rhythm. If it is the note, even the single note, which brings about existence through the purest joining of the hearer with the heard, the change which brings the joining, the marking of life, the starting time, then it is rhythm which is the "colouring of time". This phrase was used often by the French composer Olivier Messiaen, who in 1943 wrote 'Visions de l'Amen' for two pianos. The work begins with 'Amen of Creation', which encapsulates space becoming created matter letting loose an ongoing flow of existence. This music of Creation emerges from an almost inaudible rumbling bass and, over six minutes, builds through the higher registers with an insistent rhythmic urge, as the listener, enveloped, is propelled, towards… space. The end is sudden, mid-theme, but our flow of consciousness which it has evoked carries on when the music stops.

This space is not just physical and, in any way that we can know it, it is not nothing. And silence, if we could know it, would be a kind of space.

The ending of the music leaves us standing on an edge. Then we fill it with our flow of consciousness. There are moments like this when the flow can be stilled, allowing glimpses of pure experience, like shafts of sunlight through the clouds. The music, having filled our minds and ended, now silently enriches the time which follows, leaving us differently disposed to our world, without any need for our mind to replay, for in replaying we would

---

[6] If you do not have an instrument you can enter this web address – www.stillnessinmind.com/page_22.html - and press play: after a few moments a note will play on a piano - A flat below middle C - and you will be able to give yourself a similar experience.

lose its quality. These are moments of stillness and what we experience is their essence. There are others, and they are always unpredictable: the 'redness' of the sky at sunset on *that* evening, the 'piercing-ness' of the light-speed arrow of the sunrise, the way the light and shade re-created the mountain *today*, the unadorned purity of the single note intoned, like a beacon in the infinity of space and the eternity of time.

In poetry we have recorded experiences like these - the words of John Gillespie Magee, who in 1941 test-piloted a new spitfire at 30,000 feet were as close to such an experience as we can find. He started to compose as he reached the highest altitude and had just completed the poem as he came in to land:

> *Oh! I have slipped the surly bonds of Earth*
> *And danced the skies on laughter-silvered wings;*
> *Sunward I've climbed, and joined the tumbling mirth*
> *Of sun-split clouds, — and done a hundred things*
> *You have not dreamed of — wheeled and soared and swung*
> *High in the sunlit silence. Hov'ring there,*
> *I've chased the shouting wind along, and flung*
> *My eager craft through footless halls of air. . . .*
> *Up, up the long, delirious burning blue*
> *I've topped the wind-swept heights with easy grace*
> *Where never lark, or ever eagle flew —*
> *And, while with silent, lifting mind I've trod*
> *The high untrespassed sanctity of space,*
> *Put out my hand, and touched the face of God.*[7]

---

[7] 'High Flight' by John Gillespie Magee, Jr (1922-1941) from the Manuscript Division of the Library of Congress.

Remembered but not retained, these are moments with 'attachments', which stand in time outside the flow.

Such moments of transcended consciousness occur for many and in different contexts. In a devotional setting they are felt as a connection with the divine. Others might use the description of 'peak experience'. For many they are moments of removal from the flow of life happening, for which description and explanation are inconceivable because the duality of consciousness has been transcended. In the root meaning of the word they are moments of pure 'ecstasy', a standing outside one's being, one's self in abeyance. But they can never be sustained, for the act of holding demands objectivity - we must know what we are holding – pure experience is lost and the duality of our consciousness is immediately re-apparent; we are returned to the flow of living. We are returned to normal existence. But these moments of transcendence are never erased: a different kind of duality has been known: against the ground of such pure experience, ordinary living, for a while, appears dulled.

~ ~ ~

"In the beginning there was only Tokpella, Endless Space. Nothing stirred because there were no winds, no shadows fell because there was no light, and all was still."[8] So begins the account by Harold Courlander of the creation myth of the Hopi.

----

[8] "The Fourth World of the Hopis: the epic story of the Hopi Indians as preserved in their legends and traditions" by Harold Courlander, 1971, Albuquerque, University of New Mexico Press

Rising from the desert landscape of northern Arizona, extending from the Black Mesa, are four 'tongues' of rocky outcrop, the four mesas, where you will find the twelve villages of the Hopi nation. Their lands surround these mesas and, across their 1.5 million acres, they grow crops with their unique farming methods, using terraces and wind-breaks to counter soil erosion and preserve moisture in this arid terrain of minimal rainfall. Their nation wandered the desert landscape from Grand Canyon country to the Rio Grande for thousands of years, criss-crossing a parched land, bisected, but barely nourished, by the Colorado river. They gave offence to no-one, avoided conflict, were hospitable to other migrants and finally settled in their stone-built villages above the plains, the earliest of them still standing, at around one thousand years old.

'Hopi' is a shortening of a word which means 'Peaceful People'. At the heart of their culture is their reverence for Masauwu, the Caretaker of Earth, whose religious ceremonies they perform for all mankind.

Here is their story of our beginning:

"I remember my grandmother well. One day she told me that it was she who had instructed my parents that my name must be Tuwa. When she told me that, I was happier. I told her that up till then I didn't like my name, partly because it was also a boy's name and partly because it meant 'earth' and all the earth round us was dry and rocky and dusty, because we lived in what was really desert. I knew that Hopi girls had to be strong because it was our blood which stood for the Hopi nation, but I thought girls ought to be a little soft as well. But my grandmother said that I should be proud of my name because the earth was the gift of the Sun spirit Tawa, and our people were chosen to perform our dances and thanksgivings for the world on behalf of all people everywhere. That was when she told me about where the earth came from and how men and women came into being.

"My grandmother, whose name was Uny, which means 'remember', said that this world we are in now is really the Fourth World. Tawa, who is the Sun spirit was once the only being that existed, surrounded by Tokpella, Endless Space. Well, Tawa had been trying, each time he made a new world, to make it better than the one before and he thought when he had made the Fourth World that he had managed to make it perfect. I think he probably had, but it looks as though it was people that spoilt it, because when all the good people came up from the world below, they let one person with a bad spirit come up too. They knew about her, but they were being kind and that's what spoilt everything. I said I didn't see how one bad person could spoil things when there were lots and lots of good people, but my grandmother told me not to be literal because everything in a story stands for something much bigger. 'So listen to the story, Tuwa.'

"Ok, I'll start at the beginning.

"First there was just Tawa, the Sun spirit, and endless space. Tawa thought that nothing but space was too barren and so he gathered the elements of Endless Space and added something of himself to make the First World. First World had some life, but not much, just insect-like creatures who had no idea what living was about. Tawa was disappointed. So he called for his messenger, Spider Grandmother, and sent her down amongst these creatures, who were even fighting amongst each other, to tell them that they must go on a journey with her to the Second World, which Tawa had created and which would allow them to understand more about life. While they were on this journey the inhabitants of the First World gradually changed, they became more like dogs, with fur and tails and paws and this is how they arrived in the Second World. Tawa thought to himself: "All will be well here, because the creatures understand enough to feed and have families and live together in groups and they need have no cares because they do not know about death." But slowly the creatures started to fight and some of them developed in ways which gave them advantages over others and again Tawa was unhappy because it did not seem as if his Second World could be settled and peaceful.

"Again he sent Spider Grandmother to bring the creatures into a Third World. This world would be easier to live in because there was more light and more water and there was nothing that the creatures would want for to stay alive and contented. Again, while they were on the journey into the Third World, they changed - they lost their fur and the claws on their feet and their tails and they started to walk on their two hind legs, so that by the time they arrived in their new world they looked much like we do today. They found that they were able to understand about life and were able to get together and make places to live and tools to make life easier and they found out how to make fire. This was a big step because now they could be warmer in their huts and if they lit fires all around their crops they could make them grow better (for the Third World was still quite cold) and they also found that they could use the heat to make their pots harder and stronger for carrying things. Now life was easier.

"Life was definitely better in the Third World. It was

easier to stay alive. It didn't need every minute of everyone's day just to keep things going. So some people found they could do a little less, so long as others kept going to make up. And so instead of just working, some people started to please themselves and do things just for the sake of enjoying themselves. Young people started to be rude to their elders, the people who were doing less found they could take what they wanted from others instead of making it themselves, men and women no longer stayed in their own family with their partners, children went uncared for... and an evil spirit was starting to divide the people. The good people remembered how the Third World had been settled and peaceful at first and they knew that Tawa cared about his creatures, for that is why he had brought them from the First World into the Second World and now into the Third World, and so they did their best to persuade the people who had been taken over by the evil spirit to change their ways. But nothing worked and so the good people came together to work out what to do.

"Everyone wondered whether there might be another place that just the good people could go and leave the people with the evil spirit behind and one of them said that sometimes, when the air was still, he had heard a deep thunderous noise in the sky, like someone walking around above them. And then another said he had heard the same sound. And another said it was as if the sky was not the end of everything that could be seen, but that there was another place up there, another world perhaps. And so they decided to send a bird creature up through the hole in the sky to find out if there was anyone there and if there was somewhere they could live peacefully and contented.

"Spider Grandmother overheard the good people

talking and how they wanted a chance of a world where they could be at peace and contented and she went to Tawa and asked him if he would find a way for these people to go into the Fourth World, which was above the sky of the Third World. Tawa was worried about this, for, he said, the Caretaker of the Fourth World was Masauwu, who was also the Gatekeeper of Death. If the good people lived in the Fourth World they would see that everything comes to its end and that they too would die. But Spider Grandmother persuaded him to find a way for the good people to get into the Fourth World.

"And so it happened, that Tawa sent Spider Grandmother to Chipmunk to plant seeds under the hole in the sky until something grew tall enough to give the good people a way to climb up into the Fourth World. So Chipmunk planted a bamboo which would grow high enough so long as the people sang and danced to make it grow. The people sang and danced and sometimes they were out of breath and stopped so the bamboo stopped growing and formed a joint in its stalk and then Spider Grandmother said 'try again' so they sang and danced some more until the bamboo, now with lots and lots of joints, could pass through the hole in the sky. And so it was done. The Way was complete into the Fourth World and the good people could climb up.

"The elders climbed up first so that they could make sure only good people came through to the Fourth World. For five whole days people climbed up into the Fourth World until the elders thought all the good people had arrived and they called down that no more people could come and Chipmunk gnawed through the bamboo so that the Way would be closed.

"Now the people gathered around the entrance to the Fourth World, made camp and rested for several days, until the elders said that it was time for them to gather into their tribes and depart in their own directions to find their places in this new world. Tawa had sent Yawpa, the mocking bird, to give them their names and set them on their own way and he came among them and said, you will be Paiutes and you will be Apaches and you will be Comanches, moving through all the many people… you will be Sioux and you will be Hopi and you will be Bahanas, the White Men. As they were departing one of the Hopi recognised the last person who had come up from the Third World before the hole in the sky was closed and pointed her out and said she was one of the bad people. No-one wanted Yawpa to give them this person until, in the end the Bahanas, the White People said, 'We will take her. Even though she has done evil, she has great knowledge and that will be useful to us.' And the leader of the Hopi people was troubled. 'It is true', he said, 'that we do not want this person with us: to the Bahanas will come evil, but also a lot of knowledge, and so they will have secrets that we will never share and power that we can never acquire.'

"And so the tribes dispersed and the great migration started, each tribe on its own Way, journeying and settling over the whole world.'

"This is the story grandmother Uny told me and she said that this is why we Hopi dance for all people, because in the beginning we all came from the same place, the same way. 'And it's why Tuwa is such a precious name, because Tuwa is the earth and the earth belongs to everyone.'"

~ ~ ~

We need to tell our stories.

They begin in many places and happen on many levels. Individual lives, tribal narratives, histories of peoples and races - the steady march of the species which had become humans. Stand back and it can be like looking at a mountain range as dusk approaches, turning the distant landscape different tones of lavender, blue and purple, each massif a layer of deeper hue, but each one having its own place in the panorama.

We are composed from the lives of generations. Our beginnings have been many. Our awareness grew with what we touched and what touched us, changing the world with an endless procession of discovery and invention. Thence the stories. Stories of family, friends, school, work, successes, sadness, intimacies, sons, daughters... relationships all, because it is the nature of this human animal to connect.

Occasionally, though, it is alright to allow it to just be ourself alone and then, then a different kind of awareness, the paradox of a gaze which inwardly focuses on the being of one and yet still contains a beyond - the mountain range emerging out of nothing and disappearing beyond our view. Breathing in, we draw into our body the whole of creation, and, breathing out, we return ourselves to our place in that whole. The gaze and the breathing as one. In the turning, an infinite stillness.

Contemplation : on the passing which we call time

We talk of 'time' as if it is some component part of existence (rather than a reflection of it), as if it is a cog in the machine which is the engine of our being, and sometimes more than a cog, sometimes more like the engine itself. In different ways we give it form: "Father Time", "Time waits for no man".

Our means of measuring time may be absolute - linked to the rotation and orbit of the earth - but our concept of time is relative: we link it to our life-horizon at any particular moment. This comes through in expressions which incorporate it: school-days "drag"; holidays "fly by"; age "creeps up on us"; "in no time at all" the children are away and we are on our own.

In this way our concept of time is individual and personal, changing constantly, and we cannot understand it by projecting it as an external force. Time passes with us and in us.

'Time' and 'Passing'. Two words for the same phenomenon, or almost. But if we chose to, we could make a distinction: we could use 'time' to refer to the metric of seconds, minutes, days, years, and we could use 'passing' to refer to that sense which locates us in our lives, in relation to the world and everyone around us. It is part of what affects how we feel... in a situation, towards another person, about our life generally. In this way it can generate or reinforce an attitude and so affect our behaviour.

Passing implies movement and it also implies relativity to someone or something else. And so it is a recognition of change in a way that is the most individual and personal, namely in terms of our progress through the world.

Through school and college years, we are acutely aware of who is 'above us' and who is 'below us'; as parents we are maybe conscious that our children are still at home and that our friend's children have all left home and we know that events in our children's lives measure life passing; later in life we notice ageing in others and compare it to how we think we appear ourselves; "You are as old as you feel", and how old I feel is intricately connected with the scope of what I can do now compared with what I could once do, my sense of my vulnerability in terms of health, my sense of where I am now and how long I might have left. We make or resist making decisions on the basis of where we feel we are - how difficult it is to think about life insurance and pensions in our twenties!

This relativity in our passing, as a part of our living, is part of everyone else's living too. With anyone who is significant in our lives, there may be an element of reciprocality, but in the end our only referent is ourselves, where *we* started and where *we* shall finish. The latter most often we cannot know and hence the challenge of each moment nagging at us to feel and experience it for all it contains.

To Draw a Line

Take a large sheet of plain paper.

Draw the simplest line on it, just a straight line, starting anywhere and going nowhere in particular extending from one edge of the paper to its opposite.

In the middle of emptiness, form has appeared. From the reflexive stare imposed by seeing nothing, the eye is drawn away to focus on something that can be observed. And the mind follows, to formulate its response, for the 'mind's eye' cannot see emptiness, it must always see some thing. Here it sees the sheet divided by our line. When there is nothing to see, but yet the power of sight is available, the seeing is turned inward and the object of our vision is ourselves through introspection. But when looking out and being presented with an object outside ourselves, we instinctively seek to make sense of it, there is a necessity to make sense of it, to the extent that complete emptiness and complete confusion (the inability to make sense) are the same thing. This is not a discovery of modern cognitive science, for the insight goes back to the ancient Greeks with the god they named Chaos. Our modern word 'chaos' signifies complete confusion, but for the Greeks, Chaos was the personification of the infinity of space.

We have nothing if we cannot make sense, cannot find form.

The simplest of forms is a line on an empty canvas. But a line can be created in many ways. We can place another sheet of paper over but offset from the first and we will have created another image which we might also call a line. So 'line' is no longer an 'object' but a concept, a metaphor; and the question to be asked now is not "What is this?" but "What does this represent?" For if we look closely, we see that what we now are calling a line is in fact the relief become visible from a 'presence alongside'. A relationship rather than an object.

Our instinct is to form and to group in order to find meaning. With the object that we perceive ourselves to be in our body, we look first for other objects to find points of reference on the same plane of perception. We interact primarily with objects and, having defined our parameters, we set ourselves at the top of the tree! But what if we were to see the line, which creates the form which is the manifestation of each object, as a token of relationship instead of division and separation? Interestingly, it is easier to work with the sense of this in our minds than to put it into words, because the structure of language came after the hierarchy of perception. So perhaps the nearest that words can come to describing this sense would be 'the how of what one object is being to another', or, in individual and personal terms, 'the process of being me while you are being you'.

Allow for a moment that there is something to be discovered about ourselves if we detach our idea of 'line' from impressions of 'divided' or 'boundary' or 'limit', replacing these instead with 'attached' or 'touching' or 'meeting'. Now imagine a chance encounter with a slightly-known acquaintance on an evening walk, where a gathering dusk obscures clear outlines and close observation. Notice how the exchange takes on a special character. Deprived of a clear image to tempt us to make assumptions and to jump to judgement, our eyes are now the poor relation and hearing is paramount, our senses re-balancing as we listen more deeply. Our primary awareness is presence, a dimension beyond the concrete and the visual. Without clear outlines showing the other person, definition comes from a different source, more fluid, more intimate, more responsive. The intermingling of liquids of different densities and hues in a lava lamp, one outline gently ceding to another, simulates this kind of coalescence. The sinuous wave of the dark and light portions of the yin-yang image illustrates such a relationship with flowing curves of rapprochement and balance. In both, the 'lines' come into being where two different natures meet, but here the paradox: in the semi-dark of our twilight meeting, though deprived of clear vision, we can, with sensibility and patience, touch on the delicately nuanced experience of the raw human connection.

In similar vein, who hasn't sat late over a coffee or a nightcap talking with a friend as the night draws in, but neither of you having any inclination to put on the light? For to do that would be to stop the flow and break the spell of what feels like a special closeness. It is as if the darkness takes away the need for pretence or subterfuge –

"I am less vulnerable if they can't see me!" - and the exchange no longer needs the same reservation; where personal space is less apparent, the boundary between ourself and the other, which we usually visualise as a (straight) line, an image which we vest with a power of its own, now comes into being from the immediate and real exchange, escaping the dictates and distortions of our individual histories. We have less tendency to lengthy monologue, for the listening darkness imbues us with its spirit of interest and invitation, and we find we are willing the reciprocity on which relationship is founded.

~ ~ ~

A line, whether straight or wavy, physical or metaphorical, in whatever way we might express it - inside/outside, higher/lower, lighter/darker - creates a duality. On a personal and individual level, the line which represents my perimeter defines me in the context of the world - the classic duality of 'me' and 'other'. Duality means a boundary. In many situations we are conscious of boundaries, sometimes it is the duality itself that becomes obvious first, sometimes the boundary. Often the nature or the method of the presentation of information and events highlights duality and implies division - the tabloid headline which shouts "Queue Here for the Gravy Train", the commentary which reads "More immigration means yet more waiting for a hospital bed". In most cases the 'duality' is conceptual, when we allow lines, which we instinctively think of as boundaries, to create a simplistic view of the world, forming dichotomies for ease of comprehension: belonging and estrangement, kinship and outsider, native and foreigner, muslim and infidel[9].

When there is a boundary, there are three possibilities:

1. We refuse contact - physically, perhaps, or by simply not hearing, or by talking from our own platform regardless of what the other might be saying, or by offering only token communication. But there is no engagement and the situation is static. The drawing of the straight line on the page was a metaphor for non-engagement because, in creating a form out of the image, our mind was only responding internally and within the bounds of its own process: in effect it was inward-looking.

2. We accept the difference and co-exist. This goes further than token communication because we have now given the other a right (however ungraciously) to be the way they are. If the chance encounter on an evening walk had instead been during the daytime, it might have been a little like this: the lack of shared interest at a point in the day when a casual greeting might have been the norm would have allowed our two paths to coincide briefly and then diverge with no effect on either.

---

[9] The word 'infidel', which is most often today assumed to be a muslim term to denote anyone (but primarily Christians) not of that faith, comes from Latin and really means anyone not of *one's own* faith. In the 16th century it was frequently used by Roman Catholics to denote anyone not catholic. In terms of its connotation of difference and our preoccupation in the West with the polarising and often anxiety-provoking divide between Islam and our historically Christian culture, we should remember that, on the one hand, the Crusades (initiated by the Catholic church) were an early and barbaric attempt to subjugate in the name of 'the one true God', and, on the other, Queen Elizabeth I opened up England to Islam, courting diplomats, merchants and ordinary people of muslim faith, following her excommunication by Pope Pius V.

3. Dialogic relation. This is different. The lava lamp illustrates dialogic relation in a visual way, as does the depiction of yin-yang. The lava lamp with its undulating shapes from the mutual giving and forgiving of immiscible liquids exquisitely symbolises the possibility of an accommodating complementarity growing from the reciprocity of dialogic relation. The striking black and white depiction of yin-yang likewise. But there is another deeper significance. Both are depictions of a conundrum: that opposites, while separate in one sense, find their identity together.

In human relations, with our ever-present fear of incursion or intrusion, we seek refuge in separation, physical or metaphorical, and once a line is established, our instinctive need to perpetuate what is known, and so safer, fortifies our sense of identity and immutability. But we have created our own recipe for intransigence and, sooner or later, conflict. From a fear of being invaded has come formulaic communication and the impossibility of empathy. If we are tuned in to our psychosomatic responses, we can feel a tensing from the need to hold the line and then the escalator effect of the autonomic reaction which responds to the tensing with more tensing and defensiveness. The only antidote, both physically and psychologically, is a loosening, a letting go to let flow. The channel for this loosening is dialogue: first an inner dialogue, and then communication, giving and receiving, with another living presence. It happens at the line, but now the line, which was a border, is simply where it happens.

Attitude is a precursor of the encounter. Who can see where the line which traces out a circle starts, once it has completed the circumference? Our self-consciousness points up our vulnerability in the face of what is not of us and so cannot be completely known. Our anxiety about death - the 'not-being' which is beyond the reach of our consciousness - elicits a defensive response to preserve physical integrity and pre-ordains a state of mind which interprets what is encountered with doubt or even distrust: and so our vision is limited and what is seen is only what is allowed to be seen. The line as the boundary, is the absence of an open view and the impossibility of being forewarned. Security has become vulnerability; defensiveness has produced impoverishment.

It is our attitude which defines the line as a boundary and thereby overlays our perception with caution and presentiment. And if not this, then what? Break into the circle? But where and how?

The line on the sheet of plain paper was an 'object'. We focus first on objects because they can be defined and they bring an element of certainty amid the chaos of nothingness. But consciousness has deceived us. The certainty is illusory because definition stalls time. Our object is only an object in the ephemera of our perception. If we recognised this ephemerality we would not be misled, yet we cling to our objects to give us certainties and in so doing lose sight of the constant change and adaptation which is the essence of living. We fix our objects in our perception like waxworks in a museum. And yet we need not.

Within ourselves we can feel the process of our living. We can feel comfort and discomfort, tension and relaxation, arousal and boredom all in their turn. As long as we do not start to look for reasons, they remain the feelings and sensations of being alive. They change with what is around us and, especially, they respond to the presence of others. They are our living process without the intervention of thoughts and reflection and analysis. For those around us, if the same is also happening, then together we are a 'system' of feelings and responses, a meeting of living processes. Like the lava lamp, which is an intermingling of two liquids with different properties but the same nature (of being able to be liquid); with another person I might notice the differences in their character compared to mine, but I also cannot deny the essence of our common humanity, portrayed in a shared gamut of feeling and emotion. In a coming together with vision such as this there can be no line drawn, no boundary defined. In the deepest sense it is a meeting.

So here, through dialogic relation, the possibility of coming together with another human being, where the meeting is one of sharing in our humanity, an amalgam of two (or more) into one, not in the sense of symbiosis (with its implications of dependency), but rather in the creation of a new flow of being. Is this not what is happening as we sit with a friend letting the darkness slowly envelop us, while from time to time we languidly puncture its shroud with bites of conversation? But is it not also what develops when the less forthright member of the team is given space because a colleague sees her struggle and stops in full flight to make way - a group of five now becoming six?

The meeting of human beings takes place at the level of emotions and feelings, because we all know what sadness is, what happiness is, what loss feels like, what joy is like, uncertainty, anxiety, longing, regret, contentment: whatever the different sounds our languages give us to express them, our sense of them is the same. It is our minds that draw the lines which become boundaries and defences, our thoughts which take a stand in our fears and our frailties and manifest as the attitudes which become the tyrants of the engagement. And then every encounter, which could be a meeting, becomes a contest.

~ ~ ~

In central Africa, sandwiched between Tanzania and Democratic Republic of the Congo, lie Rwanda and Burundi. Their modern history since World War 2 and independence from France and Germany respectively has been one of successive totalitarian regimes interspersed with civil wars which have degenerated into genocides as the balance of power has swung between the two principal tribal groups, the Hutu and the Tutsi. Following each conflict a succession of agencies, some external some internal, have attempted by various means, judicial and voluntary, to reconcile the two communities in the interests of lasting peace and collaborative social development. More recently national initiatives at local and regional level have been informed by (but not copied exactly) the experience of South Africa and its Peace and Reconciliation Commission. But there have also been locally-inspired projects in both countries. All the experimental quasi-legal processes and innovative community effort have trusted the proposition that the line between the two tribal groups must not represent a barrier but a possibility of contact. Holding fast to the principle that if the past is acknowledged and set aside then contact can mean genuine meeting, a pathway has been opened up for relationships which draw on the present as it *can* be for each person.

There is no human endeavour which can be pursued without stumbling. All the more to be expected when we are told that the 'law of genocide' as understood by each group was that you must kill your closest friend first because if you don't then you yourself will be killed[10]. Violence turning into genocide has blighted the political history of both countries for some seventy years and in 2017 remains a very present threat in Burundi. But the process of reconciliation has been set in motion and pursued in local pockets in spite of setbacks elsewhere, and, for individuals, the steps they take are not reversed...

Deogratias Habyarimana (Hutu): *When I was still in jail, President Kagame stated that the prisoners who would plead guilty and ask pardon would be released. I was among the first ones to do this. Once I was outside, it was also necessary to ask pardon to the victim. Mother Mukabutera Caesarea could not have known I was involved in the killings of her children, but I told her what happened. When she granted me pardon, all the things in my heart that had made her look at me like a wicked man faded away.*

Cesarie Mukabutera (Tutsi): *Many among us had experienced the evils of war many times, and I was asking myself what I was created for. The internal voice used to tell me, "It is not fair to avenge your beloved one." It took time, but in the end we realized that we are all Rwandans. The genocide was due to bad governance that set neighbors, brothers and sisters against one another. Now you accept and you forgive. The person you have forgiven becomes a good neighbor. One feels peaceful and thinks well of the future.*

Laurent Nsabimana (Hutu): *I participated in destroying her house because we took the owner for dead. The houses that remained without owners — we thought it was better to destroy them in order to get firewood. Her forgiveness proved to me that she is a person with a pure heart.*

Beatrice Mukawambari (Tutsi): *If I am not stubborn,*

---

[10] Testimony of Jean Paul Samputu: 'The Forgiveness Project', 2014

life moves forward. When someone comes close to you without hatred, although horrible things happened, you welcome him and grant what he is looking for from you. Forgiveness equals mercy.[11]

Some doubt whether the sense of one community which has largely pervaded Rwanda since President Kagame's decree in 2003 that most genocide offenders be released if they confessed and asked for pardon, will survive his tenure and become his lasting legacy. Can you change attitudes by decree? We might question that. But the counter question is also valid: if we keep to a path alongside another, even if only through acquiescence, could it not become a life?

---

[11] From an AMI (Association Modeste et Innocent) project by Pieter Hugo & Susan Dominus for New York Times Magazine.

Lost and Found

We're very good at looking for differences; we're not so good at looking for similarities. Think about those occasions when we are introduced to someone we have never met. Quite naturally it is physical appearance which we notice first and unconsciously we skip through a number of comparison checks - male/female, older/younger, bigger/smaller, dresses like me? speaks like me? - and if we were to slow this process down we would notice that the checks which produce similarities go unremarked and those which produce differences lodge in our mind and often produce their own subset of exploratory questions. Almost as if we were *looking* for the differences. Unless we stumble on something we have in common and which particularly engages our interest - do you play football? do you have a family? - but even then the comparison routine picks up quickly and once more it is the differences which are being noticed.

What drives this noticing of difference? Does it come from a need to be 'one up' and therefore feel secure? Does it come from a need to find differences in order to be sure of who we are ourselves?

And what is the outcome, for each of us individually... and for humankind as a whole?

The Silk Road is the name given to the ancient route for trade and migration which started from the Bering Sea in eastern China and ended in the Levant (modern Lebanon) at the Mediterranean, along the way passing through Uzbekistan Tajikistan Afghanistan Iran Iraq Syria. For hundreds of years it was our planet's most important highway with a span of over 4000 miles. Because it was a trade route across lands which have been witness to innumerable conquests and upheavals and migrations for communities and nations, it is peopled by many different races and ethnicities. But for all this, and despite 2000 years of upheaval, there are more similarities in the bloodlines found along the Silk Road than there are differences.

Always when we look across the sea, over the mountain, down the street, to the other side of the road, we first notice difference.

Primeval man - the original fully conscious human being, the neanderthal world's version of the man on the Clapham omnibus, the anthropologist's *reductio ad unum* in the interests of clarity of focus, the originator of the human race - would have struggled to comprehend this, though he might have seen his part in the unfolding drama. Alone in his hunting ground he would have wondered what he was. He could have looked at a rock and known he was different from that because the rock was hard and lifeless; he could look up at a tree and know that this was not him either because, though it appeared to be living, the tree was fixed where it was; he might have looked at an animal - which was certainly closer - but the animal was bent over, its head was at the end and it propelled itself with four limbs not two. But then coming down the hill opposite there was a creature moving on two limbs with two more limbs waving around independently and with its head on top and he felt elation because now he knew what he was, he had found his likeness. "I am one of them!" As the creature approached, though, he probably felt a nagging uncertainty: definitely a superficial likeness, but looking closer, differences as well. These differences added to his uncertainty, for if there were differences he could see, there may be more he could not see, and differences he could not see might spell danger. In any case there was a need for wariness and caution and possibly even to fight or to take flight.

Thenceforth our species' instinctive (well, almost) noticing of difference before likeness.

Might we try to break this more or less autonomous process? Not of course by denying differences, for that would be futile, but by recognising similarities or the possibility of similarities. And if we *were* to break it, even on the odd occasion, what then could be the effect? Though if we don't even notice that it's happening anyway…

> *"It's five thirty and I'm on my way home.*
> *Automatic pilot at this stage, it's the way I let the*
> *stress of the day subside, head down, no need to*
> *think because I've done it so many times, ten*

minutes walk to the station, two sets of pedestrian lights, check the board in case of delays or a platform change, none usually, I don't have to stop walking, platform 6 at two o'clock from the concourse entrance, the train waiting, touch my card on the reader, third coach down usually the best for the time I arrive...

"Sitting opposite me a youngish guy, twenty something, looking out, confident, dressed flamboyantly but smart, very smart, young executive, own business? He must be tall, long legs, stretches out, surveying the scene, looking for a pretty face? I feel a bit insignificant, conventional. Even his briefcase, thick black leather, large man-bag style, initialed. No tie, expensive shirt unbuttoned.

"This girl next to me, she can't take her eyes off him. His hands, plain gold ring on his right, no ring on his left hand. What's she thinking - available? I'd be surprised if he was."

What feelings are coming up as you sit there in that carriage? Envy? Longing? Self-deprecation? Resentment? Most of us have been there and we can rehearse it all - the misconceptions, the faulty thinking, the unsafe conclusions - yet sitting opposite the young man on the 17.30 to Milton Keynes, it would still be differences that would come up first for most of us, even though we would be able to re-think the scenario and come up with similarities. If we tried, we could replay the scene in our heads from a similarities perspective and then we would notice how much better our experience was.

We might be inclined to make light of this. Differences? Similarities? Just personal choice. But the world, our society, our work group, are all made up of other individuals, and at all points of contact we have the same choice - to notice our differences or to recognise our similarities. So where could this lead - this new perspective, the noticing and flagging of similarities first? Only everywhere. For if we are noticing similarities, we are unlikely at the same moment to be registering differences. That is the nature of our dichotomous thinking. And there are spin-offs from that. With a perception of 'similar' goes a leaning towards the positive, in the way that our thinking works. In place of threat comes possibility. Which feels more comfortable. Now, as my face relaxes, I will appear more open. Now, if he were to look my way, that young man on the train, and make eye contact, there could be an exchange. No longer just him and me apart, for now there is also this shared 'space' in the middle which relational therapists call "the between".

In the field of human relations, the concept of the between is elemental. It has no physical form, yet both parties are stakeholders. We could go as far as to say that when two people are fully and genuinely engaged with one another, psychologically, for that period of time, they cease to exist as individuals and exist *only* as the between, as the flow of what is passing between them, which is their relationship with each other during that while. It could also feel as though the between has a value which extends beyond what can be observed as a 'moving between', for it contains an investment by each person of a part of themselves, and then, as with investment of any sort, comes that innate human reluctance to disinvest, to disengage. As if there were some kind of magnetism present. Perhaps this is an element of the gambler's urge - "I might win more if I stay" - or the worrier's instinct to only foresee the negative - "without this I've got nothing" - but there is also the warmth that comes from making a connection, and a realisation that we are only fully human in association with another.

Similarities, communication, connection, and then there opens up the whole field of interchange, not just at the micro level of two individuals, but over all fields of human encounter, through to international relations and cooperation. The processes which operate for each of us individually extend within our society and extrapolate to the society of nations.

~ ~ ~

Perhaps we might wonder how this unmediated reaction of noticing difference originates, because, insofar as it is a cognitive process, and so might appear to 'just be there', it will have a source and an explanation somewhere else in our system.

When we see difference we are using two components - our perception of the other and an awareness of ourself. Both of these use consciousness.

Consciousness is what distinguishes us from all other species (to the best of our knowledge) and it is both a blessing and a curse: a blessing because it is the source of our ability to reflect and conceptualise (from which comes our power of invention and so the advancement of the human species); a curse because it lays us bare to the ravages of anxiety. Consciousness gives us the awareness of ourself. It means that we do not just feel but we know that we are feeling; it gives us the means of noticing what is us and therefore what is not us.

And there it is - the fundamental stage of the process of comparison, the noticing of difference, as a simple binary element of me / not me. In this way the primary functionality of consciousness in separating 'me' and 'not me' privileges the noticing of difference. To change this around so that similarity was privileged would threaten the whole basis of our existence because it would dissipate the instinctual boundary-making which allows us to distinguish ourself from the world surrounding us.

Yet there is also a perversity in this default of noticing difference first. Our awareness of difference does not just mean that we know ourselves as who and what we are, that is, to have an identity in our own minds, it also brings a sense of separateness. Separateness is double-edged: it not only allows a sense of security because it chimes with individuality, that symbolic holy grail of the Western mindset, but it also raises the spectre of isolation and loneliness. And, whilst it is true that standing out from the crowd is mostly seen as a virtue, at least in the West - the heroic independent spirit - at the same time, being subsumed into the symbiotic mêlée of a like-minded throng has its comforts too and keeps at bay the bleakness of being one.

Loneliness, aloneness, isolation, have different resonances for each of us, but they all draw on that same basic aspect of our makeup, that not to have connections with others is not a normal human state. You could say that, up to the point of extinction, it is not a normal state for any species. Biology determines that. But for us, more than for any of our co-habitant species, it is not normal because the basic currency of our existence is our nuanced form of thinking which allows our communication by speech. It is speech, or rather the thought process which underlies it, which allows us to hold in our minds ideas about others which facilitate our 'other' responses of empathy and projection.

Does it seem strange to put empathy and projection together as responses to others, given that they seem opposites in the context of human-ness and fellow-feeling? Empathy, after all, contains an attempt to share how things are for the other, whereas projection is an inadvertent and unconscious misunderstanding or misapprehension of the other for our own greater comfort. (In its conscious form it is abuse and, if pursued deliberately, manipulation.) But the theme here is loneliness and its antidote is connection, any connection. Enemies can gain mutual respect and even become friends. The sworn antagonists of the violent conflict in Northern Ireland, Ian Paisley and Martin McGuinness, did not simply acquiesce as co-leaders in government after the Troubles: after a while they became genuine friends. It could not happen until there was contact and communication, and this, in turn could not happen until each discerned some similarity in the other. Certainly, political pressure played a part, but so did the commonality of an exhaustion from the stalemate.

At our own personal level, too, we can find that someone with whom we are very guarded or to whom we are instinctively averse, seems less threatening or disquieting when conversation happens.. Which comes first, the observation or the conversation? Whichever it is, it is an intention formed from a will to look for similarity which offers the possibility of a 'between' and the opening up of another of life's cloisters. Aloneness assuaged.

We can be alone in a crowd. And the desert does not need to be an empty stretch of sand and rock. Loneliness can be within us and *its* desert might be the aridity of relationship disowned.

Jean-Yves Leloup[12] suggests that we can never escape the desert...

> ... it is what remains of our love when living disconnects it from the most tender attachments

> ... it is what remains of our most lofty thoughts when age and forgetfulness has erased them

> ... it is what remains of us when time claims our gage

> ... it is what remains of our faith when it is dissipated in the face of unaccountable reality

A Desert of Disillusion

We have big words to describe the presence and effect of strong emotions... we talk about a *tide* of emotion, being *overcome* by *waves* of emotion... expressions which paint a picture in which the images depict surge and strength. In the picture we see movement - the word 'emotion' itself means a 'moving forth' - and our eyes paint with a broad brush shapes of swell and irresistible force as, from inside somewhere, we feel the surge of impulse and give ourselves over to its clutch, becoming possessed.

There is a deceptive simplicity about this.

The metaphor of the big picture and the stunning images bely the intricacies of the everyday dealings of human interaction, which are both the source and the

---

12 Jean-Yves Leloup, "Désert, déserts", Albin Michel, Paris, 1996. I have altered the wording, the imagery and the examples, but not the sense of Leloup's themes.

antidote for our strongest emotions. Love, anger, loss, hate all involve relation, if not with an individual then with a collective. Multitudinous threads connecting us through a welter of individual exchanges. But we have a disposition to be possessed by emotions, which results in the emptiness we feel when their source is removed. And then the desert of an absence of possession. Anger, when exhausted, leaves a feeling of disconnection, hate when dissipated leaves a flatness of spirit, loss when the yearning is passed leaves dullness, love when used up can leave disillusion. Strong emotion is all or nothing and the nothing is void of the intricacies and banality of everyday existence. We have been wooed into believing that it is only in the drama and the passion that we really experience what it is to be alive, whereas in reality it is as much the connection and mutual exchange with the world outside our emotional cocoon, which is the stuff of living.

The traveller who has survived long wearying days of passage across the dunes and plains of Rub'al Khali, the 'Empty Quarter' of the Arabian peninsula, after 800 miles of nothing but sand and arid bone-dry bedrock, at first barely notices the specks in the distance. But gradually they are there, tiny interruptions to the impersonal naked line of the horizon. The heat haze evaporates and mutates the minute aberrations, but slowly, as the miles are covered, they take form, these specks, and grow into blocks, link together, acquire colour-tones which separate them from the desert, and then they stand as buildings and people-gathering places and start to pull the traveller toward them.

Loss, grief, despair, disillusion are conditions which bring a dulling of our receptiveness to what is going on around us. The sense of pointlessness which they contain shifts the perspective. Perspective contains a valuing because some things are always preferred over others; the shift in perspective re-arranges this and devalues what exists, in the shadow of what is unavailable. We stop connecting with what we no longer value. The horizon, which is all around us, flatlines. We are in a desert. Until, out of the gloom and the brume appear the specks, the aberrations, a touch, a word, the feeling of the grass, a glint of light barely noticed, but something was there… and now again. Slowly, very slowly, this desert of the soul recedes. Like the colours differentiating shapes out of the formless expanse of sand, living re-kindles our essential energy and starts to pull us through.

A Desert of Inconsequence

There is always more that we do not know than that which we do. What we know is finite; what we do not know is infinite because its limit is unknowable.

And who is it that would do the knowing?

At the heart of the ego is a conundrum: the person that I feel myself to be seems to own himself as a knowing 'I', but there is little that is of me in what I own. My physical being is the end-point of a genetic chain and my way of looking at the world the residual of the nature handed down to me and a wayward progress through my life's events.

The answer to the question "Who am I?" can only be "'I' is another"… until we can say "I" with no illusion about the person who is uttering the sound. For confirmation of our existence we search for an image of ourselves, but the mirror is broken and we gaze into a cluster of cubist shapes which hint at the whole, while they dissect the soul.

This is the desert without an end, for to reach the end would render the question inexistent, evaporating in its own answer. 3500 years ago on a mountain in the Sinai desert Moses asked of God a name, and was told: "ehyeh ašer ehyeh"... "I am that I am". The answer, handed down to the creature made in God's image, that nothing more can be said? Or the answer, projected by the finite on the infinite, that nothing can ever be known?

A Desert of Estrangement

Something changes for us when the possibility of death by a cause which is present and knowable enters our world. Be it a potentially fatal diagnosis or the immediacy of extreme danger, the perspective with which we see the world, others, and, most of all, our part in the ongoing drama, changes irrevocably. Even if the danger passes, our perspective never returns completely to what it once was. The continuing presence of what we know - people, things, places - does not diminish this sense of desert, of life having been "left waste" (to use the Latin origin of the word).

Our overriding sense of life is of living, an experience of being in our bodies and responding to what is around us. Living is a process and the nature of a process is the linking of activity from one moment to the next: inherent in our being alive is our expectation of continuation. Death, of course, changes the game-plan for good, but the 'concrete' possibility of dying does not go this far, though it still alters perception. We realise that, until this point, the future has been built in to our sense of being alive, and that this, the expectation of a future, is something we share with everyone else. Implicit in each moment is that there will be another and another. It enters into our consciousness and is part of our experience of existence. Until it is in the balance. At that point, the sense of a future is no longer something we share with others, and so we are set apart. As if separated from the momentum of living by a glass screen, we are apart from all those others for whom the end is not in sight.

It is a strange place we then inhabit, though it has its own kind of peace. Free from the pressure of needing what is happening to have ongoing significance, we now look out on a world which is at once simplified, as when an artist might draw his subject over a colour wash of its rough outline, but it is also thrown into relief, its form intensified by the background of colour. No longer striving for purpose, we are in the picture and we are observing it at the same time. It is the 'milieu' of our existence, but it is also separate from our existence. We become observer and observed, estranged from that aspect of our life which was once fundamental though unacknowledged - its continuation. The desert which we now inhabit is at the same time bleak in its prospect and comforting in its simplicity.

A Desert of Emptiness

It seems to be a part of human nature to want to put faith in something or someone outside of ourselves. Regardless of the object of that faith, the faith itself, the belief it contains, the trust that is its manifestation, all fulfil some function for us. Is it a projection of the anxiety that our uncertainty and vulnerability causes? A comfort blanket? Or does it come from an acknowledgement of ignorance, as a response to our need for there to be a complete answer somewhere so that there is the possibility of perfection? Or is it from a need to know that there is a purpose and a meaning to an existence which can stimulate us and inspire us, but can also lead us into despair?

This desert, though, is not in the faith, but in its disappearance, for here there seems to be no parallel with the popular wisdom - "better to have loved and lost than not to have loved at all". The loss of faith feels more existential: love, in a sense, is a choice, but faith, when it is present, feels like a necessity. Perhaps a safety net: "if I can't believe in something, then there's no point in all this". It is conventional for non-believers to say that God is a projection of humankind's death anxiety and search for meaning, but this desert of emptiness does not arise in the loss of belief in a particular deity or belief system, rather it comes from the nothingness itself, the absence of any ground on which faith might persist. The nature of faith is 'all or nothing'. In this way it presents a dichotomy which is a rigid divide, accentuating difference and boundary and postulating certainty as quasi-knowledge, when nothing is actually known. Certainty acts like a drug and like most drugs, dulls the senses, making us vulnerable. It takes up space in our life. It brooks no questions, it re-writes the meaning of our experiences in its light. Certainty gives comfort, and faith is the blanket. To have faith is a way of living, a way of being. Faith may endure, even to the end of a life, but if it is lost, then the way is open to desolation and aimless wanderings in the desert.

Yet it is of the nature of faith to waver, because it is *not* knowledge. It is a voluntary yielding of reason, and contains belief and trust. Its realm is not that of the mechanics of day-to-day life, though its effects are likely felt there. It has a vulnerability in that it is subject to the unmediated assaults of life events: the possible assailed by the actual. So the person of faith wavers, whether their faith is in a godhead or the world or themselves or humankind: for some their faith returns and for others not. We are a long way from knowing how the mechanism works - whether it is in the nature of the individual, or the object of faith, or the circumstances of its loss - that one person may be restored in their faith and another not. But after a revival, it will be seen as the constancy of the faith object from which renewal has come.

Just outside the village of Tibhirine in the Atlas mountains south of Algiers is the Cistercian monastery of Notre Dame de l'Atlas. Since its founding in 1948 - it was the village which grew up around the monastery, rather than the monastery which was implanted in the village - the monks ministered to the community, providing medical care, teaching in agriculture and giving informal general support. Alongside the Christian monastery the village grew, a Muslim community, and each was respectful and caring of the other.

For a Cistercian monk every day begins at 03.45 and the day consists of six offices in the chapel, with afternoons set aside for work and ministering activities. Lives at Tibhirine were dedicated to the following of this path of faith, which was manifest in the ceaseless obedience to the ritual of the day and devoted assistance to the villagers who lived alongside and around them. All of life was ritual and service: your fellow-brothers were your family and your life had already been given.

In 1996 one the monks living at Tibhirine had been there since its founding in 1948. He was the doctor among them and was 82. For two years the community had been aware of the constant danger to their lives as more and more foreigners were assassinated by the GIA, a militant group fighting for the removal of all vestiges of Algeria's colonial past and to replace a corrupt government. But the brothers took the decision to remain.

On the night of 26th March 1996 seven of their number were kidnapped and taken into the mountains. After failed negotiations by the GIA to secure the release by the government of one of their leaders, on 21st May, the monks were killed.[13]

Only the monk who had been at Tibhirine since its founding and another brother now remained. They had escaped notice at the time of the kidnap. But their world, their family, their lives of ritual and service had ceased to exist. In such a world of 'afterwards', 'before' evaporates as if it had never been. And in this desert, for Amédé and Jean-Pierre, also the desolation of a survivor's guilt.

All who have lost someone close have looked out across this desert. For some there is a long time wandering in the wilderness, all the while knowing, seeing even, the world beyond, but always beyond reach, in the distance. For others, living starts again sooner but changed, as we always are changed, by tragic experiences.

Likewise a faith that has been shaken may sometimes slowly be restored. For Amédé and Jean-Pierre it came

---

[13] The circumstances of their deaths and the recovery of their remains is a matter of dispute, but that is not the purpose in telling the story here. The monks' graves are at Tibhirine monastery, which was finally re-opened, though not as a monastery, but a shrine and a place of pilgrimage, with one sole monk-guardian.

with their eventual arrival at a sister monastery in Morocco, perhaps helped by the words of their now dead Friar Christian de Chergé, who, in a statement he wrote and read to his brothers as the inevitable approached, spoke of his end, when he would say thank you and adieu[14], even to the very man, his killer, into whose eyes he would be looking as his life ended.

"Et toi aussi, l'ami de ma dernière minute... je te veux ce MERCI et cet "A-DIEU"... Et qu'il nous soit donné de nous retrouver, larrons heureux, en paradis, s'il plaît à Dieu, notre Père à tous deux. AMEN ! INCH'ALLAH !"

("And to you also, friend of my final moment, I wish this thanks and this goodbye... And that it might be granted to us that we may find each other again, happy vagabonds, in paradise, if it pleases God, the father of us both. Amen. God willing.")

---

[14] The French word 'adieu' or 'à-dieu' means 'to God'.

Contemplation : on the discovery of emptiness

These words are from Mechthild of Magdebourg:

In the desert, turn toward emptiness;
Fleeing the self, stand alone,
Ask no one's help, and your being will quiet,
Free from the bondage of things.

Most of us most of the time are conscious of 'the bondage of things'. Which of us does not at different times feel constrained, by routines, by obligations, by our culture, by work, by relationships, by surroundings, even by the person we are? Mostly by the person we are.

Always the age-old problem, and that most crippling impediment of the human condition, that the mind which is seeking release is the mind which is locking the door. The prisoner and the gaoler are one.

Always the fear that if we let go of the clutter of things, release ourselves from what we want to believe are simply the superficial trappings of a shallow existence, we will find, not the deep and comforting wisdom of the ages and the fulfilment of being at one with all around us, but instead just emptiness.

'Nothing' is not a thing that we readily comprehend. It was millenia after the dawn of civilisation that there was a symbol for zero: consciousness decrees that there is always 'one'. And our dominant awareness - of being - means that 'not being' is inconceivable and that death is just a word, a projection of now into an indeterminate beyond.

But still the desert offers hope. And it offers a means. For the desert is a world of primary experience. A stark landscape of primary colours and harsh contact. Where any attempt at projection is foiled, for nothing can be engraved on its landscape of shifting sand, and every sound is stolen by a restless wind.

Primary experience.

One question only.

What matters?

All Real Life is Meeting

These words appear in 'I and Thou',[15] the iconic work of the man we know as Martin Buber[16]. He was philosopher, anthropologist, sociologist, and he was also a very prolific writer. He was not the only early twentieth century thinker to develop the theme of Man's relationship to Man in the way that he did – the revelation that it both reflected, and and was itself reflected in, the dialogue he has with others and was defined by how he says "I". But whilst Buber's philosophy falls broadly under the banner 'existentialist',

---

[15] 'I and Thou' was described by its author as an ecstatic utterance and the first of three quite short parts contains the essential insights by which he is most widely known. It was written and published in German in 1923 and first published in English by T&T Clark Ltd (Edinburgh) in 1937. There have been other English editions, but this first one, translated by Ronald Gregor Smith, has the feel of the poetry of the original German, reminiscent of the King James Bible.

[16] Mordechai Buber, an Hasidic Jew, was born in Vienna in 1878 and died in Jerusalem in 1965. He was a leading light in the revival of Hasidism and a protagonist for a post-World War 2 state in Palestine in which power would be shared equally by Jews and Arabs.

the poetic style of 'I and Thou' and his insistence on dialogue as the process at the root of Man's existence, marks out his contribution as not only the most profound, but perhaps also the most easily engaged, of this school.

This chapter is grounded in the ideas of Buber, set against our experience of life today and its realities in our century.

~ ~ ~

When you first had life you were part of your mother. When you were born you became physically separate, but from instinct sought to re-establish the connection - you needed food and comfort - whenever proximity permitted. As your consciousness of being separate began to form, you started to act out your emerging personality. As you grew and discovered more about what it meant to feel distinct from your surroundings, you realised that you had wishes and urges and that you could act on these and that this often led to your feeling better - and also often got you into trouble! As you progressed through childhood, alongside the self indulgence of simply wanting to feel better, you started to notice how others might contribute to your feeling better and how you could often set this up. And you started to recognise what it was like to feel pleased with yourself.

In adolescence, bewilderment and turmoil: how to be safe without being stifled - for there were always times you wanted comforting; how to break out without being broken up - the conflicts of idealism and a burgeoning ego. The arena of self-belief and self-doubt carried through into young adulthood with a dimly-perceived sense of a strategy for survival in a disinterested world. The need to control... something. And so the impulse to construct a view which complements your insecurities.

Do you take a risk? Or do you ensure you are well-defended? The chess player seeking to manage the board, the player of Go looking to surround and neutralise and dominate.

The game comparisons are allegorical, but in their way they reflect how Buber described our sense of the rest of our world when we adopt our customary way of viewing what is around us… that everything is (or can be) 'our domain'. "But *I* didn't try to neutralise anyone or control anything", I am sure you will be saying. And you would probably be right if we were talking about how we deal with a physical world. But in reality *[sic]* we are not: we are talking about how we behave outwardly according to the version of our world we carry around in our heads. The difference between that world, our perceptual world, and reality, the physical world, doesn't often occur to us and rarely bothers us. Just the stuff of geeks and philosophers, you might say! And it may be, and it may not matter… but then we find ourselves getting worked up and upset about an absence of politeness in day-to-day life, or worried about the effect of social media with the licence it gives for unbridled nastiness, or angry when our voice is not heard and distraught when we are thwarted in trying to make a difference… and we are falling into the trap of thinking it is all about someone else. From the tee-shirt slogan "I love the world, it's people I can't stand" to the famous quote from Sartre's play 'No Exit', that "hell is other people", our default line is that the problem is 'out there'. And seeing it as 'out there' may occasionally be accurate, but that is still no help in trying to make the situation better.

It is rather trite to say that it's all a matter of how you look at things, though that is certainly a good starting point. And whilst we might not go as far as Sartre's character in saying that it is *never* situations which cause us problems but the people involved, that too is nonetheless instructive because it focuses us on the fact that our most difficult psychological struggles relate to people and their actions and very few to impersonal events or circumstances (acts of God apart).

We are moving towards the unavoidable and perhaps uncomfortable recognition that it all begins with what we mean when we say "I".

It is a well-rehearsed observation that if two people watch the same scene unfold from the exact same place and are then asked to recount what happened, their accounts will be different. Such a unique and individual perspective has advantages and disadvantages. If we are looking to make up a picture to include all the elements of what has gone on then it is an advantage, but if we are concerned to know the exact sequence of events in order to determine cause and effect (and maybe responsibility), then it is more likely to be a hindrance. There are two factors in this, which are not completely un-connected: we select what we think is important, and how we do that depends on an amalgam of experience and conditioning - we process the information we *can* process, the data that our frame of reference gives us the means to interpret. If we prefix each of the accounts of the scene witnessed with "I saw", we can start to get a sense of how facts - at least what are called facts - are not so much universal as individual. Without manipulation or conscious intervention, we are defining and controlling them. And if we think of facts less as defined circumstances or events and more as our belief about what is happening and how, then we start to get a glimpse of the extent to which we make the world work in our way - not the hard physical reality of what happened when it happened, but what it has meant to us, which in turn leads on to how we deal with it.

The process of perception is a process of putting our stamp on something. With any or all of our senses, we receive what is outside us in the process of being confronted with it (or her or him or them). But this is not perception. Perception comes after the sensory nerves have passed their data to the cerebral cortex, and is the process which interprets and re-writes that sensory data in a useable form for thought manipulation. The process of interpreting is also a multi-layered operation. Almost everyone would look at a tree and say, "That is a tree"[17]. But beyond that, there would be very little correspondence even in descriptions of the physical features. Some would remark on colour first, some shape, some size, some would notice the leaves, before even encountering the significance of trees in their own life - climbing as a child, a fall, Christmas, getting lost in a forest, deforestation, rain forest, logging, sheltering, and on and on. Each with our own unique combination of description and meaning, we put our stamp on it. For everything with which we come into contact, we hold a 'definition' in our head, culled from multifarious sources, which is likely to affect even what we 'see' as we look, for the process of recognising a thing is a process of matching the data we receive to the data which

---

[17] It is interesting to reflect on that which is the essence of something being what it is: in pictures of World War 1 battlefields we still call the blackened denuded pillars, trees; we still call a person who has lost all their limbs, a person.

we hold. If there's a match, we don't have to look any further... we don't have to *think* any more.

A story is told about a nobleman who bought an elephant to help some villagers with hauling timbers for repairing their houses after a bad storm. When he arrived in the village the only men who were there were those who could not be out in the field working because they were blind. Never mind, he thought, my servants can show each of them the elephant and they will be able to see how it can help them. So his servants had each of the blind men feel a part of the enormous creature... one was led to feel its legs, one its trunk, one its tail, and so on.

Later the nobleman called the men together and asked them how they imagined the elephant and how it could help them. They all looked uncertain about how the elephant would help - the one who had felt its trunk said the creature was like a tree branch, the one who had touched its tail said it must be a rope, the one who had felt its belly said it was just a wall, the one who had held a tusk said it was a solid pipe.

The nobleman was disappointed because he realised that in some way everyone could be like the blind men sometime, seeing a small part of something and thinking they knew everything. And if they would only share what they could each see, then much more could be achieved.[18]

Whenever we hear something or look at something and say to ourselves, "that is so and so", we are taking a

---

[18] Versions of this story are told in many traditions. It seems to have originated in India and many versions have Buddhist settings, but not all.

snapshot. It may be what we say it is at the moment we say it, but a moment later it could be something else... *will* be something else, because nothing stops changing.

So here we have the downside of our faculty of perception (which comes from our unique attribute of consciousness) - we never see a thing as it is, rather, we are always seeing things as they were. Perhaps, as they were only a second or so ago, but still as they were. Add to that the fact that we interpret what we see in a way which makes it unique to us and we can begin to realise that reality, actual physical reality, is not something we can ever hope to know.

Double bind: we have snapshots only, of a world which is changing, not in digital slices, but in a continuous analogue flow. And even our snapshots are only partial images of a world twisted round to fit our preconceptions.

The utterance of the single-letter word of existence, "I", the "I" that sees, configures the domain in which we move and have our being, and it also determines our behaviour, through the illusion of reality we are acting on.

Consider for a moment an encounter in the street, a young man slightly dishevelled running towards you, looking anxiously over his shoulder as he runs, some disturbance behind him, it's not clear why, but something says - danger, keep away - and you step aside to let him through, his general appearance imprinting itself in your mind, but only afterwards seeing he is being hotly pursued by two store security guards. Now later, another street, a different young man though similar in appearance (that image of the first one still in your mind), but here sitting on a bench and looking anxiously from side to side - 'shifty' you think, up to no good, and walk away, leaving him alone. But this time 'shifty' was actually dazed, and he was shivering from shock after a hit and run accident.

Or the new member of the work team just transferred from another department. You have heard she likes to 'nitpick' the details, which holds up meetings as she insistently - some say belligerently - goes over each and every clause and statement. And, true to form, this is what happens at the first meeting and you get irritated, because you like to keep things moving, and then defensive, because a small slip in some figures of yours is uncovered. You snub her at lunch and then again later in the day. It's a couple of days before you're inadvertently standing alongside her at the coffee machine and she notices your trainers because her partner's got some like them and she wonders which club you belong to and you say and she thinks that you and he would get along... and you check your figures twice before the next meeting because you want it to go ok and you will feel better about it then anyway.

Small beer, but sometimes big consequences. Always out of date, we too often hold on to what we 'know' until forced to update the 'facts' - from just now, from yesterday, from last month, last year, from what we 'always knew', the latter entrenched in assumptions and prejudices and attitudes for which we would have to rummage to even find the key.

This "I" that is calling the shots can get in the way.

But what if there were another way?

What if we could allow the rest of our world to be just what it is, knowing that the closer we can come to seeing and being seen just as we are, the greater our chances of being at peace with ourselves and others; because peace does not come from everyone conforming to our ideas, but from the complementarity we bring about with a process of negotiation and understanding based on full and genuine disclosure?

~ ~ ~

In linguistic terms the "I" which was implicit in everything that has gone before in this chapter is the "I" which is the subject of a transitive verb. Everything which isn't 'I' is an object: even if I say "You have red hair", you are my object, whether or not "I" appears in my sentence. This is the "I" which Martin Buber calls 'I-It'.

But just occasionally you may be able to detect a different sort of "I". As when two friends are walking thoughtfully along a path that they each know from different encounters and in different circumstances, and one says to the other "this isn't easy, I guess, so many memories" and the other looks over and simply nods.

Buber called "I-Thou" the version of "I" in which we are able to acknowledge another person for everything about them, even without knowing everything about them; and let them be ok as they are, even without really knowing the basis on which we say "ok". It is the ultimate in trust by one human being of another, but goes beyond the dimension of the person to the level of process, affirming that it is in the relating to another that our very world is being created; that it is the nature of the 'between', which comes about from this act of relating, which both contains and creates our humanity.

The 'Thou' of 'I-Thou' sounds archaic to us today, but it is the expression chosen by the original translator from the German. Since the modern English pronoun 'You' is the same in both subject and object, singular and plural, he returned to old English for a form which was uniquely subject. It was important because, when we feel ourselves I-Thou, as 'I' I am the subject of my sentence, but I am bringing the other person also to be the subject, and thereby on the same level as me, no longer my object.[19]

So what is in the I-Thou? "Just everything", says Buber. Except, necessarily, liking the person to whom you are speaking. This maybe seems paradoxical at first, until you realize that it is about doing a relationship, not doing a friendship (necessarily). And it is about universality and inclusion and not about selectivity and grouping. It will always be relatively easier to be amicable and accepting of peers and associates and like-minded people, but for Buber an understanding of I-Thou and its indivisible link with the fundamentals of being human goes beyond that. In our era, if we chose to heed this way of genuine dialogue and respectful encounter - the 'meeting which is real living' - from this man who was respected at the United Nations and advocated a state for post-war Palestine with equal rights and status for Arabs and Jews, then we might, we just might, discover the pathway of peace.

Genuine dialogue demands an absence of preconception and prejudice, an absence of agenda with regard to the other party, an absence of *expectation* about the outcome of the encounter. It predicates an openness and receptiveness to the other which goes beyond active listening and acknowledges her or his validity in terms of ideas feelings and emotions, and the integrity of their existence as another human being.

---

[19] Unfortunately recent translations have adopted 'I-You' and have therefore lost this subtlety.

But the ability to conduct genuine dialogue does not depend on words alone. In fact it depends little on words, for the practise of genuine dialogue makes no reference to content. It is possible to conduct a conversation from our I-Thou and not be in agreement with the other person, even perhaps dislike them. For genuine dialogue depends on attitude not on sentiment. If I am fully allowing the other person to be ok because I share their humanness, even though I don't like what they are saying, our dialogue can be genuine, because I am hearing just what they are saying without the distortion of my prejudices and the blur of my conditioning.

For most of us, simply to set aside prejudice, just because we know we ought to, is a hard ask. To un-blur the view we receive through our imperfect conditioning is near impossible. Many hours, after all, are spent in therapy seeking to undo the many ways in which our past encroaches on us and limits us. To do this moment to moment is surely implausible. Certainly it is, if we are seeking to block or hold in what has simply come into our mind, unmediated by intention or will, and unimpeded even by our desire to be here and now in the present. But that is not the way. Instead we must follow the first and most primitive impulse of being human - to connect. Again like the first human, alone in the world, seeking to understand what he is, knowing that he can't be a stone, or a tree or a wooly mammoth, who looked up and saw his likeness coming towards him, and felt the relief of recognition with the possibility of connection. True, anxiety sets in as the likeness approaches and doubts for his safety start to arise and so he takes a stance; and now the impulse to connect has metamorphosed into the need to be on guard. His likeness is now his object; he has reverted to 'I-It'.

Here is our challenge: to enter into genuine dialogue we must draw on that primary impulse for recognition and contact, before the spectre of separateness, with its undercurrent of isolation and its depiction of the other as an 'object', intervenes and drags us around to face a world for gain. And if we do, if we achieve that moment of real connection before the comparisons, on which our consciousness insists, intrude, to describe the experience as exhilarating would be no exaggeration. Such a moment of connection has a beauty like no other. Rilke recognised it in lovers' faces, before they are clouded by the world:

> *Lovers, if the beloved were not there*
> *blocking the view, are close to it, and marvel...*
> *As if by some mistake, it opens for them*
> *behind each other ... but neither can move past*
> *the other, and it changes back to World."*[20]

But it is not just the prerogative of lovers, it is the entitlement of anyone who chooses to claim it. Who does not yearn to mean something - to others, to mankind, for themselves? Who would not respond to a gesture, which may not mean friendship, but carried genuine recognition and acceptance?

This being together, this recognition of each other, needs no magic, though what flows from it can feel

[20] From Rainer Maria Rilke, "The Eighth Elegy", translated by Stephen Mitchell in "The Thunder Mutters", ed. Alice Oswald, Faber & Faber Ltd. 2005

magical. It is not a skill which has to be arduously learnt, rather it is a facility we already possess and only need to uncover:

"At first I found it bewildering the idea that 'I and Thou' could apply in so many different places where it was me and other people. The most moving for me was with my daughter. I thought we had always been quite close - occasionally I had done a long holiday trip with her and she came to see me weekends and I had always tried to be the steady father, not interfering too much and ready when she needed me. But then there was this party, she was in her teens, and I guess she saw me as she wasn't used to seeing me and after, when everyone had gone, she went wild with me. She was very angry. I didn't know what to do she was so angry. And I just opened up and told her lots of things about me, good and bad, perhaps mostly bad, well real anyway, and afterwards she said - "I've always known you as your work and stuff and all the time you were this figure… now I know you're a person, not just a figure". And since then it's been different between us. Like a different sort of invisible connection has been made.

"And then at work, there was a meeting of all the departments and these things are always pretty difficult for me. This time the same and what was getting to me was that everyone was closing themselves off, all in their own boxes just talking about things from their own perspective and it was all so dry and sterile. It wasn't going anywhere. I don't know how it happened for certain, perhaps I looked at someone some way, perhaps I picked up

something someone said, but I know I came in with something I was enthusiastic about and they could see I was fired up, not like they usually saw me, and suddenly it was all different and everybody was listening to each other and even to me, and they went away with my idea about working together in a whole different way."[21]

~ ~ ~

And so to meeting, for this is what true dialogue really signifies, that two people have encountered each other in the nakedness of their wishing to be just who they are, being known in the encounter simply and completely as who they are. Meeting through true dialogue opens up a realm of opportunities which most of the time we can only occasionally light on. There is no pretence, because in wishing to hear the other in the fullness of their real self and opening to them to allow this to happen, we must set aside all guile and artifice. This congruence, though, between internal and external, between willing something and manifesting it, can come naturally into being from a focus on the other which allows them to be co-subject of the process, through our letting be and listening, through our presence alongside their presence. Then, with the meeting, comes undistorted contact and an exchange which can fashion true accord, not necessarily without compromise, but with mutual appreciation.

What defines a meeting? An offer and an acceptance and then an offer back. Without the offer - even if it is no more than the welcoming face which says "I am listening" - then there cannot be acceptance, and without the

---

[21] Account of a client at *Le Sentier Tranquille*, the author's retreat centre in the French Pyrenees (with permission).

acceptance there is no reciprocity. To say "I understand" is not enough unless I am listening to the whole person and hearing not just the words but also the meaning and significance of the words for their speaker. It is the inclusion of the other, as they are, in my world, their 'Thou' alongside my 'I', whether or not I agree with them or even like them, that makes their response and offer back reciprocal and sets up, even if only for an instant, the mutuality of true dialogue.

And such instants can now be created again and again, because we have uncovered the process, we have found the key.

~ ~ ~

The reach and scope of true dialogue extends through the whole domain of human association. There is no context in which we cannot envisage an outcome elevated by the sense of mutuality which comes as the exchange unfolds. Who cannot relate a time when a word which resonated, or a look exchanged with caring eyes, broke through social reserve and connected us, even if only for an instant, with a knowing of "yes, that's where I am too"?

From the private and everyday to the public stage of international dealing, beneath the veneer of diplomacy and bravado of political posturing, lies the possibility of a connection which transcends the divisions that appear through difference. For boundaries need not be lines of demarcation and estrangement; boundaries can also be meeting places. And what it demands is not the betrayal of hard-won individuality, but the espousal of genuine fellowship: equal actors in a shared space.

Ubuntu - I am, because you are... or the nature of geese

I have always had a fondness for geese.

I say always, but I am not really sure when the fondness began. It doesn't feel like it would have been a cool thing for a lad in his teens... though he was a lad in his teens long before anyone talked about "being cool". Perhaps it was when I first came across Paul Gallico's 'Snow Goose', the evocative story of a boatman-artist; who is brought a wounded snow goose by a young local girl; who nurses it back to life as their friendship blossoms, and the snow goose flies off each summer, returning later in the year; who is lost with his boat in the evacuation from Dunkirk... and the snow goose returns one last time. Rather too sentimental a story, you would think, to grab the average adolescent, though I do recall a deep emotional vein in me even then, which seemed a foil to my rather reasoned and sober exterior.

No matter, somewhere I picked up the notion of the relentless onward urge of a flock of geese in flight - arrow-like formation, honking their encouragement to each other - an unstoppable forward momentum. So that many years later, while driving in Scotland I was bewildered seeing two white geese fly over the road in front of me and then, a couple of minutes later, turn and fly back, crossing my path again, in the opposite direction. Around the same time I read William Fiennes book 'The Snow Geese', which describes his journey following the 4000-mile migration route of those geese from Texas to the wilds of the Hudson Bay in Canada. It was thereabouts as well that I first offered to a client Mary Oliver's wonderful poem 'Wild Geese', in which she likens the harsh and exciting call of the geese in flight, to the way the world calls to us "over and over announcing [our] place in the family of things".

The closing lines of that poem hint at the remarkable characteristic of geese, which enables birds with an implausible power-weight ratio to migrate 4000 miles in such a short time. They do it together. Physically together, yes, in a large flock, but not just that. Their close-formation flying pattern means that the draught from each bird's wings gives an uplift to the bird behind, which reduces that bird's energy consumption, thereby adding around seventy per cent to the range of the flock as a whole. But what about the leader, you may ask? It will surely die of exhaustion. It probably would, if there were one, but there isn't really a leader, just the bird at the head for a time, and this position rotates: the bird at the front goes to the back after its turn and then starts to move up the order again. And if a bird drops out, two more drop out of formation to fly with it, support it until it is strong enough to resume, or wait with it until it dies.

Single-minded - to reach the destination.

Co-operatively organised - to benefit collectively.

~ ~ ~

Ubuntu (long before it was the name of a computer operating system) had been an indigenous working philosophy across most of sub-saharan Africa. "I am, because you are"; "I cannot be me, unless you are you". For people speaking Bantu languages across southern Africa (Ubuntu is the plural of Bantu) this encapsulates the spirit of co-dependence, co-operation and community which is in the blood of Africans of all tribes.

Bill Clinton expressed its essence in a typically insouciant way: "If we were the most beautiful, the most intelligent, the most wealthy, the most powerful person - and then found all of a sudden that we were alone on the planet, it wouldn't amount to a hill of beans."[22]

Desmond Tutu incorporated Ubuntu into his theology in order to demonstrate that a peaceful displacement of apartheid in South Africa was possible. In 1992 he went so far as to say: "A self-sufficient human being is subhuman. I have gifts that you do not have, so consequently I am unique. You have gifts that I do not have, so consequently you are unique... We are made for a delicate network of interdependence."[23] For Tutu, Ubuntu, with its message of the community of all people, was a way of drawing on innate qualities of the African as the embodiment of New Testament teachings. He observed that Africans have a synthesising mindset as opposed to the occidental

---

[22] UK Labour Party Conference 2006

[23] Desmond Tutu, "God's Dream" from 'Waging Peace", Nuclear Age Peace Foundation, Santa Barbara, 1990.

analysing one. In the fearful climate of South African apartheid, an ubuntu theology offered a means for the oppressed to humanise the oppressor without giving away their belief in their own value and humanity. The bold statement that my being depends on yours and yours on mine transcends moral judgement because the relational paradigm precedes and pre-empts the moral one and the dialectic of Ubuntu is existential. The statement of its essence is as stark as the black and white curves of the yin-yang image. And its message is as simple: individual living can only be experienced in context and the context is community… and ultimately humanity.

All easily-grasped concepts run the risk of being hijacked in the service of trendiness or fashion because their simplicity belies their depth. Mindfulness, which could be said to complement (but not replicate) Ubuntu, is also an example of this. Its essence is no more sophisticated than to pay undistorted and undistracted attention to what is actually present, but it has fallen prey to phone apps and jargon. Ubuntu in its turn has been lauded as a methodology for running all manner of organisations in order to avoid the failings of a politics of materialism and the myopia of short-term solutions. But its implications are more profound than the implementation of a method of management, for which its name has been evoked. Mindfulness, Ubuntu, Person-centred, Koinonia - these are neither merely formulae nor techniques nor even simply regimens for living, they are philosophic kernels. In philosophy they can be fundamental to the branches of ethics and politics, but they are also implicit in metaphysics. So, we can feel them as part of our nature, independent of the world around, and elemental in our belief about the possibilities for humankind. And, if we so choose, we can install them as part of our way of acting and being in the world.

Along this pathway, we move into the intra-psychic domain which we might loosely call 'attitude'.

Our attitudes account for so much of what we do and how we do it. (Along with our anxieties.) Attitude, used almost as an expletive, has sometimes come to be thought of as being negative, a way we might have of putting ourselves across a little too forcefully, something about us which others find discordant. But really we can use the word to describe our frame of mind and approach in relation to anything - which might find negative, but also can find positive expression. So, attitude in relation to mindfulness, an attitude of mindfulness, would indicate a *way of being* which noticed and attended to what was present and immediate inside and out: it might include a plan of action for where we were going, but not loosely-related or unrelated thoughts. If this mindful attitude were a default way of being, such a person would come over as attentive and flexible, open and engaged. In other words, unmediated by conscious intention, the default of being mindful would have become their natural disposition.

And so it can be with Ubuntu.

For Westerners Ubuntu seems to demand a conscious intention to initiate an action, in a way that it does not for Africans. That is not to say that the simple definition - 'I can only be me, if you are you' - references any conceptual blind-spot for a Westerner, even if it might necessitate a pause for thought. If anything, for Westerners, the proposition calls up too romantic an image of togetherness, where the romance hails partly from an uncomfortable awareness that it is so rarely achieved.

Neither, for Africans, is it to say that Ubuntu is not a philosophy in action, but simply that for a Westerner it is not instinctively an attitude as it is for the African.

The story about the American anthropologist studying customs in a village in South Africa is enlightening on this point, even if it is apocryphal, for it is typical of experiences of many visitors to tribal communities. He wanted to gain popularity among the children to help in the work he was doing and so he placed a basket of sweets under a tree and told a group of children that when he said "Go" they could run to get them and the first one there could have the sweets. He lined them up and said "Go", whereupon they ran shambolically together, picked up the sweets and shared them out. When he asked one girl why they all stayed together when the first one there could have had all the sweets, the reply was, "How can one of us be happy when the others are sad?"

But Ubuntu is also more subtle than this. In the yin-yang field, it is the 'meeting-ness' between the black and the white. It is the token of existence and the script of the co-creation. Saying this is not to imply an ethic of equality born out of any sort of communist-style idealism. Ubuntu in its purest expression is not a dogma or a morality, it is a philosophy of the nature of existence. It has been convenient in different situations to attach a moral, if not a political, message, but these are not its essence. Its essence is the dependency it expounds - "being me depends on you being..." - and the co-creation which results - "so that we both may be".

Moral and political extensions have come at different times and in different forms. Marxism could be interpreted as an Ubuntu-style movement to reinstate a sense of mutual benevolence and dependency in the vacuum which followed the disentitlement of a society's wealth accumulators. In the traditional African tribal court system a different arena of indissolubility is recognised: punishment for the offender is linked to restitution for the offended in the form of payment in kind - a restorative justice which is absent in Western courts, where punishment is retribution and the tie between perpetrator and victim is lost.

We might also make an oblique comparison with the attitude to 'favour' in many Eastern societies. Guanxi is central to the maintenance of cohesion in traditional Chinese social organisation. It has its origins in Confucianism and is founded on a principal of reciprocity - the obligation to repay, when a debt, through a favour, has been created. Such a notion of obligation, or more specifically indebtedness, though in Western ears it rings of uncharitableness, nevertheless maintains an ongoing relationship between the two parties, and in fact the debt may not be paid for a long time, if ever. In contrast a favour that is simply a gift, forms a connection only for a moment. In society's terms there is no lasting bond and therefore no continuing basis of relation. In individual terms, for the recipient, it risks worse than this because a gift accepted through necessity can engender resentment in someone who feels demeaned by the implication of charity.

Perhaps the practice of Guanxi has the feel of a system imposed, where Ubuntu feels as if it arises from the nature and instinct of peoples who are used to being part of a tribal society. But even that is to take a moral stance. This being human demands another and it is the *maintenance* of this contact with the other which is primary and vital to the practise of humanness: the *nature* of the contact then comes into play and gives working form to the social structure which evolves.

Again, for those of us from a Western culture, perhaps there is a struggle, once more, to set aside a sentimental bias. Steeped as we are in a christianised culture and captivated by the notion of 'goodness' as freely giving, we look askance at the proposition that holding in debt can be a positive element in how society might work. Yet in the New Testament too, in the Parable of the Talents, we find more than a hint at the appropriateness of maintaining social stability through obligation and relation. In the end, though, it is difficult to be sure whether it is our bias towards giving without strings, or our strident individualism, which is more liable to hold us hostage.

Ubuntu as a force for changing society can only come from an individual attitude which becomes widely dispersed, an attitude which has to arise from a sense of our self as being *incomplete*. Once more, in a Western culture the notion of 'individual' and 'identity' are so strong that such a proposition is almost incomprehensible. From Plato in his *Phaedrus*, where we first see duality appear as physical/metaphysical, body/mind, through Descartes with his famous words 'Cogito, ergo sum', 'I know, therefore I am', we have been inculcated with the vision of the singular 'I'. 'I' is self and whether or not we feel satisfaction in our self, it is what we are and *all* of what we are (in a non-physical sense). In the 2000 years which have been dominated by Christianity and Islam the completeness of the 'I' has been reinforced, though now the loop incorporates God or Allah. We are either completely subservient to the will of the deity - "If Allah wills it" - or only acceptable (to obtain salvation) if we place ourselves at its mercy. But whether it be submission or salvation, it predicates wholeness, with the individual self bound to its construction of the deity, and in this way, complete and sufficient. The necessity and expectation of salvation in Christianity, viewed from this perspective, is insistent: "Verily I say unto you, inasmuch as ye have done it unto one of the least of these my brethren, ye have done it unto me."[24] God and man in spiritual conjunction.

But we are children of our culture and being irrefutably whole is inseparable from our idea of self: in being who I am there is only 'I'.

From this starting point Ubuntu is a challenge to the very fabric of the self, because we would have to re-write our definition of being; we would have to allow that 'I am' must always contain 'We are'.

So what do we have to dismantle in order to make such a statement in good faith?

In practice, almost everything.

We could bring an African slant to how we think about this. In our neighbourhoods and our communities there are many groupings, which we might call tribes insofar as they are set up and arranged around a particular purpose or objective and presuppose allegiance to it on the part of their members. In the same way that early tribes came into being through a common need for protection and survival, which then furthered the emergence of a shared identity and broadened the range of activities they could achieve in common, so we too organise ourselves to support our communities, to promote ideas, to manage our resources. In any locality, even outside the sphere of religion or

---

[24] St. Matthew's gospel ch25 v40

politics, there are likely to be interest and pastime groups, whether that be a football club or drama group or knitting club, and as well there could be groups for campaigning and for the maintenance of community facilities. And then there may be branches of larger tribes, even national tribes, the WI, Rotary, Red Cross, Amnesty. Anywhere that we use 'group' or 'association' or 'club', we might also loosely use 'tribe'. Each has a sphere of interest and the spheres intermingle, because the human character is multi-layered and, in this respect at least, can multi-task. And so, in this sense of 'tribe', we are all likely to be part of more than one.

But the human character also has a significant streak of self-interest, which to a greater or lesser extent we all struggle to set aside. It manifests in different ways, but always betrays a vulnerable part of us. The 'hierarchy of needs' set out by Abraham Maslow in 1954 in "Motivation and Personality" is still a valid framework for helping to understand this (even if we might now cringe a little at his exhortations based on studies of "exemplary people").

So, paraphrasing Maslow's model, in the beginning we must survive physiologically - we must eat and drink - and then we must stay safe - from natural hazards and potential predators. After this we need to belong - partner, family, tribe, nation - and then we look for esteem in our various spheres and within the tribes to which we belong. Finally (at the top of the hierarchy pyramid) we seek to live and give scope to everything that we are - a process known in therapy circles as 'self-actualisation'. It is at the level of these two top layers - looking for esteem from others and our self-actualisation - that our way of knowing ourselves is different... and that conflict with an Ubuntu attitude will arise.

Working up the pyramid again - once we have sufficient to feed ourselves, our attitude is invariably collaborative, because protecting ourselves is always more effective if undertaken with others. This leads naturally to a sense of belonging. So far, in our thinking and exchanges, 'we' is likely to have been more common than 'I'. But now, in seeking esteem, the 'we' transposes to 'I' - I may still be listening to others, but now I seek to cultivate them as well, in order to enhance my sense of belonging and improve my position perhaps. Finally, in the realm of self-actualisation, the interest and the focus become purely reflexive.

In belonging to the tribes of which we are a part, there is a lot of 'we' in the energy that we devote to them, but they are also avenues for our private pursuit of the esteem of others, as well as vehicles for the actualisation of the person we believe ourselves to be. So often we have a need to be noticed, and there are many ways we find to self-promote: always volunteering and constantly being the source of new ideas are both laudable and beneficial, but a belief that we are somehow thereby indispensable to the tribe comes from the ego's neediness and distorts the tribal dynamic of equality in the pursuit and realisation of the community-agreed purpose.

Cue Ubuntu. And what are now revealed are those facets of human nature which will need to be moderated, if not sublimated, if this philosophy is to take root. In place of the strident voice which holds forth without check must come the sensitivity of the ear which registers others' contributions and comradeship. In place of the assertiveness of the prime mover must come the solidarity of the co-traveller.

For *one* cannot be fulfilled unless *all* are fulfilled.

Would this mean the end of any momentum for improvement? Or could the initially less tangible benefits of solidarity, the feeling of worth and the energy from making common cause, become the impetus for the crowd factor, become contagious and shake the foundations of our materialistic mindset?

Around us in the twenty-first century we have a web of communication like at no previous period in history. To some extent it contributes to making the early part of this century the turning point that it is. For the advent of near instantaneous global promulgation of 'news' means that no action of war or insurrection can take place without a countervailing reaction, no polemic go unchallenged, no cunning unexposed. And social media, which is a part of this web, can also galvanise opinion to a cause, orchestrate public displays of support and mobilise popular movements to an extent hitherto unknown. Here then is a channel for a rolling out of Ubuntu worldwide. Malign influences and manipulation apart, social media offers the possibility of worldwide human exchange on an individual level, which is the basis of relation and the starting point of Ubuntu on a global scale...

So long as we listen at least as much as we speak.

For how can I know that you are able to be you unless I allow myself to hear you? Ubuntu requires engagement and engagement begins with *receiving* and only afterwards passes to response. Responses can come in many guises: at the level of one-to-one, 'liking' and commenting a social media post is a connecting response; 'sharing' a post has the potential to expand the tribe. But the ripples can go much further: the possibility of promoting causes for charitable and community ends has been demonstrated many times over.

The philosophy of Ubuntu is now being invoked as an organisational method for agencies and businesses in many spheres (not just softer and not-for-profit projects) and the thinking could be seen as an extension of the trend in management theory that has been happening over the last couple of decades - the trend for flattening the traditionally hierarchical structure of business organisation in favour of teams co-ordinated by team leaders. The byword for many today is 'collaboration', which is often thought of as a synonym for Ubuntu. But its sense is not identical and to think of it in this way is to short-change Ubuntu. The intention of any commercial or charitable organisation is to further an objective - the financial gain of the shareholders, or the wellbeing of the target recipients. Collaboration in this context is invariably to achieve a decision-making process which ensures that everyone's ideas are heard, everyone's work is recognised, and that a path chosen has constructively and effectively taken note of each contribution. The potential is that each member of the tribe feels fulfilled in the part they have played in the shared project. In a limited way each member of such a team, could see their part as a practice of Ubuntu, if, in the sphere of their common purpose, each can feel their share of satisfaction and fulfilment.

But outwith Ubuntu as an organisational mantra, for all of us as individuals its implications have the potential to be more demanding.

Boyd Varty, who with his family owns and runs a game reserve in South Africa tells a story of how his life was saved by one of the reserve's trackers, Solly Mshongo.

Tracking one day with him on the banks of a river, he had waded into some shady shallows without seeing the crocodile which was lurking there. It attacked, clamped its jaws over one leg and proceeded to lift and shake him and pull him into the murky water. He managed to strike a blow at the belly of the crocodile, which released him and retreated into the shadows and waited. His leg was mangled and he was in waist-deep water with the crocodile between him and the safety of the bank. Solly waded out from the bank, through the shallows in which the crocodile was still lurking, lifted Boyd over his shoulder and carried him back to safety.[25]

We might all be able to relate to the Ubuntu nature of Solly's action - that he could not have been whole again if Boyd had died that day - but probably not many of us would have waded into those shallows without hesitation, as he did.

Ubuntu, on an individual level and as a personal way of being, is also my *need*, in order to feel whole, that my neighbour be OK.

Perhaps there is only one sphere of our existence today in which the practice of ubuntu as a personal way of being is unquestionably critical: the wellbeing of our planet. Here, our interest in our neighbour being OK is identical with our own self-interest. For if the planet cannot sustain its other children, it cannot sustain us, and we will have betrayed our children and our grand-children, and squandered their world, with which for a short while we had been entrusted. For this reason – for the survival of our children's children's children - if for no other, we have to walk hand in hand.

---

[25] TEDWomen talk December 2013

~ ~ ~

It is said that there is an African tribe who, if one of their number does something wrong, will take him to the centre of the village where the whole tribe will completely surround him. Then for two days they recount to him all the things he has done *right* in his life and all the ways in which he has been good, because everyone - this is their belief - comes into the world good, but sometimes makes mistakes. Their mistakes are a cry for help. In this way of helping, the tribe are bringing the miscreant back to his original true nature.

Perhaps the story is apocryphal in its detail, but its spirit comes through in the traditional Zulu greeting:

NABAJYOTISAIKIA - "I respect you, I cherish you, you matter to me"

SHIKOBA - "So I exist for you"

Love's Path - wishing to give and willing to receive

In the beginning...

"If music be the food of love, play on"[26] is probably the most quoted line of Shakespeare, but also most often quoted with an intention different from that of Shakespeare's character Orsino. Orsino hoped that, with a surfeit of music, as with a surfeit of food, his appetite would be satiated and he would find relief from his frustration. In everyday usage today it is more likely that we are imputing an aphrodisiac quality to the bard's suggestion of music's role. but Shakespeare's connection of music with the inner processes of love points towards something which has always fascinated us and might help to enlighten us.

Hélène Grimaud, the French concert pianist, author and

---

[26] The opening line of 'Twelfth Night'

environmentalist, writing in the preface to her CD 'Credo', also seeks out the link between music and love. She takes us into the very process of that connection which happens between composer, performer and listener: "Ce n'est pas le musicien qui compte, ni la musique non plus. L'auditeur seule, et cette étoile qui se lève, inattendue et impossible, dans le ciel de sa tristesse; la chaleur dans son froid; l'espérance inconnue dans l'océan connue et tourmenté du désespoir. L'amour est là. Ni dans celui qui donne, ni dans celui qui reçoit, ni même entre les deux: il est l'échange de l'un à l'autre." *(It isn't the musician that counts, nor is it the music. Only the listener, and the star that rises in the firmament of his sadness; warmth in his cold; the unfamiliar hope in the familiar turbulent ocean of despair. There, is the love. Not in the one who gives, nor in the one who receives, nor even between the two. It is the exchange from one to the other.[27])*

... the question

'What is love?' can be the question which is not asked (because it is rendered superfluous by a tide of emotion sweeping aside all rational process), it can be the expression of a yearning to counter disillusion. Here we may sense a lingering unease. Our confession of that inner stirring - 'I love you and I am in love with you' - both releases and enslaves us. Like taking the cork out of the champagne bottle - it releases the pressure which was there all the time in our hyper-tense and erratic behaviour that was threatening to burst out and shatter our socially adaptive exterior, but, once released, what is let loose is a part of us that we can never reclaim. And so the enslavement - for we have a vested interest in staying

---

[27] Translation by Richard Evidon

whole, but now there is this part of us, part of how we know we are alive, part of our consciousness, which is still connected to us, but which is no longer completely under our control.

What matter? We are in love, with all the delusion of certainty which goes with the absolute conviction of that… and this is where the shadow reappears. With absolute conviction comes a kind of megalomania, a belief that if *my* love is strong enough, then that is all it needs for *our* love to flourish. This megalomania is the breeding ground of confusion. And hopeless longing. And jealousy. And desperation.

… *the word and the music*

Perhaps the problem is the word, or at least the many ways and senses in which we use it. And, just perhaps, the clue really *is* to be found in music. Love, suggested Grimaud, is not even something which sits *between* two people, rather it is the passing from one to the other. Let's extend this idea: we may sit alongside another in silence, be they good friend, family member, or beloved, and we 'know' them in our mind, and we may notice a stirring inside us, but love itself, Grimaud would suggest, only comes into being in the exchange between two people - a look or a touch or some words, like a melody created and being heard.

So is it only in the expression of love that we create a place for it in our world? That would be a purer concept altogether than our customary confused notion. (Ironically, the etymology of the English word 'love' is closer to this meaning than its French equivalent 'amour'. Our English word has very ancient roots in Sanskrit and Indo-

European languages, which convey a *process* of pleasing and caring, in other words, something being exchanged. 'Amour' on the other hand has a much later source which conveys a sentiment rather than a process.)

... and what grows from exchange

We could try this out together now, if you like, this sensing of the process, as you sit reading.

Think of a piece of music you know and like and that fits with your mood of the moment, and now let me be with you in your mind playing it for you - I play the piano and so it would be in a piano version. You are listening to a piece which resonates with you right now and will evoke, perhaps memories, perhaps images, perhaps thoughts and feelings, in tune with how you are in yourself; but it also evokes something else, which, though it may be similar, will not have been with you in the silence before the music began. Before the music began there was the 'state' of how you were and how I was; and then the music, being listened to, being played, transforms these for us both. The process of transformation has as its catalyst the sounds which I am creating and we are both hearing and which will influence but will not predict where you and I will eventually arrive.

Music, a touch, a look, our words, they all have a donor and a recipient: all are catalysts of transformation, all have an intention and an outcome and a sequel (because process is continuous) and they are given meaning by all three of these.

As I play to you, I want to share, not just the sounds which the composer has given to the world to do with what it will, but also the part of me which creates a meaning for me in the sounds; as you listen, the same sounds find a place in you where their meaning for you evolves to kindle your response.

And if it were not music, but a touch or words, arising from what I thought was a love I felt, could it truly be love just because I felt it? Or can love be only that which wakens the heart that would be wakened? Can we truly say there is love, unless love comes back?

... *the enduring between*

If love is what passes between us, it is not something that resides in me and which *I* would therefore own, or resides in you and which *you* would therefore own. We bring it into existence together, but in giving it life we cannot claim ownership of it for we are no more than custodians of our part of it. Like the composer writing their score, who has to hand it over when it is done and can make no claim on the music which is created from it or the response it evokes (for notes and staves are no more than the seed from which the plant grows), and must leave for others the living experience of the performance: we too can only live in love while love is living.

Then is there nothing that can be expected and nothing that can be trusted? How can it be that myth, legend, and history itself, have so many accounts of love surviving prolonged separation?

In Greek mythology Aphrodite, the goddess of love herself, conspired to prevent the union of the beautiful mortal maiden Psyche with her own son Eros: offended by mortals who found Psyche more beautiful than herself, she sent Eros to ensnare her as the husband she can only know in the dark; one night Eros, believing himself betrayed by Psyche, leaves, and Psyche has to endure Aphrodite's wily tests before she is reunited with her beloved.

The many legends which surround the destruction of the city of *Wilion*, (also called *Ilium* and *Troy*), were immortalised by Homer in the Iliad and the Odyssey, and include his epic account of Odysseus' journey home after the Greek victory, to be reunited with his wife Penelope. Through the 10 years of the far-off war and the 10 years of Odysseus' journey home, she had fought off suitors to stay loyal to her husband, though having no word of his possible return.

In 1741 Jean Godin des Odonais in a Spanish colony in South America married the 14-year old Isabel Gramesón. Several years later he decided to take his family back to his native France following the death of his father, and he left his wife and children in Peru in order to investigate how safely to negotiate the politically complicated journey. After 20 years without news Isabel was told of a boat waiting to take her down the Amazon, (on the other side of the Andes mountains), and she set out on a journey to reach it during which she encountered mountain, forest, disease, death and desertion and from which eventually she emerged the sole survivor, finally reunited with her husband in 1770, 21 years after she had watched him leave.

And today, still, many know the torment of an agonising wait for the return of their loved ones from overseas military postings.

Somehow the music is heard when the notes aren't sounding.

~

What is love?

Its essence is in the love of a mother for her child. All other loves aspire to this but none can reach it, for it is without preoccupied self or cloying sentiment. It is what christianity saw as the fundamental quality of God, though a patriarchal society meant that God would be male. It shares the *I-Thou* of the mystic of Hasidism[28]. It knows the moment when meditation transcends self. As an essence it *contains* nothing. It is only being.

You can hear it in the harmonics of a deep-toned bell; you can see it in the stillness of a mountain lake, blue with the unclouded sky; you can sense it in the space that unites the clusters of atoms which form us; you can feel it as warming in the depth of your being.

Love... again

When I say I love you,

it's not because I wish the wind would gust and lift the chiffon of your summer skirt for just a fleeting moment...

though maybe I do...

---

[28] Martin Buber

When I say I love you,

it's not because with trembling hands I'd feel your naked shoulders, my nervous fingers stroking, reaching for your neck...

though maybe I would...

When I say I love you,

it's not because I've dreamt of you, drawn your tender body to me in a perfectly complete embrace...

though maybe I have...

No, when I say I love you,

it's because I want to share with you the innermost place in me, where hide those delicate outrageous trivial precious thoughts of nothing much at all...

and want to know you want me to.

... and again

Rare as the wild pearl
in crusty oyster shell,
unconditional love

~

... with its many layers and many facets

The spectrum of love is broad and the gamut of its machinations diverse.

Who does not want to be held special? Who does not want to mean something to another? The token might be no more than a passing greeting casually offered, but which nevertheless shows our presence has been noticed. Or, at the other end of the spectrum, it might be our own intentional exposure of our inner self, laid bare because the other's knowing of our darkest secrets is a collusion which brings the relief of exculpation.

From the mother's love for her child, to the long-term companionship of a deep friendship, to the intimacy of a committed romantic relationship, there is a thread running through, which reveals and explains the fervour and vulnerability we feel in the face of this emotion we call love. We may, with Grimaud, be able to say that love is the actual happening of the exchange between two people, or we may want to look on 'love' as something that resides in the being of each person - love as an emotion.

But for each individual who is a participant in the dance we call love, there are likely to be conflicting layers of feelings. This love, which we want to regard as a sentiment that arises purely from the generosity of our spirit, in fact has a darker underside, which hails from the investment we make and the risk we take whenever we connect with another human being. For any moving out from our self-contained state of being involves an opening up of ourselves, and each opening is an offer to the other, which, once made, has to be honoured.

In such a primordial transaction there are only two responses - accept or reject - and acceptance, with the discovery that the offer was genuine, ignites the fuel of trust which provides for continuity.

In opening up, we are offering from our 'me' that which we could, if we wished, have chosen to keep enclosed and protected. But once our offer is accepted, a part of us has gone; a part which, because this is no physical exchange but a venture of the soul, can never be recovered.

... *and its reticence*

Once, in order to capture some local colour, I was taking some photographs in a market square in North Africa. After a few minutes I became aware of a disturbance on the far side of the square, for which I seemed to be the object, and I saw a group of Berber women calling and gesticulating, waving their hands in front of their faces. For these women, my camera was stealing something they had not freely given and which they needed to protect. Some years later, in a more remote location, I asked my host, a Berber man, what I might photograph around the village without risk of causing offence. He replied that the women would not want to have their pictures taken... "and perhaps," he added, "don't even *look* for too long."

The significance of the face, physical and metaphorical, is something which we find in different forms but in all corners of the world. There are native Americans who believe that to be photographed is to allow one's soul to be stolen. Those Berber women who would not risk being captured by my camera even from across the street, though muslim, were not acting according to their religious beliefs, for Berbers rarely cover more than their hair, but rather from a more instinctive fear of losing something inalienable from their being. In our own culture and language, we find expressions like 'losing face' which have their origin half-way round the world in China, where the three words for face in the physical sense have different metaphorical connotations - personal esteem, respect, prestige - each compound expressions, which, in the nineteenth century, gave rise to 'save face' and 'lose face' amongst the English community living alongside the protocol-dominated culture of China.

Our response to losing something we have not freely given is alarm, anger, perhaps even panic, for it represents unexpected and unwanted encroachment where we were vulnerable. And that same sense of vulnerability persists even when it is we who have invited the encroachment, when it is we who have made the offer and made the first approach. Vulnerability in the moment, to being rejected; vulnerability ongoing, because we have entrusted this part of us to another, on whose acceptance we now depend... for ever.

For what is known cannot be un-known and what has been seen cannot be un-seen... and so much passes just with a look, without even a word being uttered. A look makes a connection which begins a process and the process creates a 'between'.

... and its beauty

Beauty is a between. We think of 'things' as beautiful - beautiful people, a beautiful landscape, a beautiful building. And we also say that beauty is in the eye of the beholder, which suggests that it is a perception. But perception arises at a time and in a place, and how the beauty is seen (or heard, or imagined) also contains what the perceiver puts into it of themselves, not just its own physical properties. All of these elements will be different at different times. So what is beautiful at this time may not be at another. Today I might stand in awe of an imposing cathedral, tomorrow, standing on the exact same spot, I could be anxious because I feel its massive solidity as threatening. Beauty is a phenomenon of coincidence: a joining together of what is around for the perceiver and what is offered by the perceived.

And there are more layers. What is around for the perceiver invariably contains projection. We can see this in the most simplistic of examples, the comic sketch face of the emoticon which we select to represent our unstated feeling, but which we use to elicit a complementary response from the other side. In our sub-conscious mind we are constructing a response in tune with our present wishes.

And so with love - the impossibility of purity.

Echoes of Kierkegaard here, though his version is perhaps even more challenging: "...the paradox of self-love is awakened through the love of another... Self-love lies at the foundation of, or goes to the foundation of, all love..."[29] In our own mundane ways we confirm this, for who, in saying to their lover "I love you" is not willing the same words back, a response to confirm that we in turn can be loved? And is this not self-love?

So also, for Kierkegaard, with Christian love (and Kierkegaard was a devout Christian) - "Love thy neighbour as thyself", which predicates that self-love must come first.

Love then is the coming into being of a process which springs from each individual as they are in that moment

---

[29] Søren Kierkegaard "Philosophical Crumbs" [244], first published 1844

and in some way contains all their desires and dependencies, their wishes and needs. We could say that the nature of that coming into being is characterised by these same desires, dependencies, wishes and needs. Its intensity as well. Setting aside lust - we will come to it next - the strength of the love impulse will depend on the needs of each and only to a *lesser* extent on the physical attraction of the other (because we have set aside lust). Neither is need absent as a component in altruistic love, for the more my 'love of giving-without-strings' becomes a part of the way I lead my life, the more it is how others see me and how I might see myself, the more it is part of my identity for myself and for others, and therefore the greater the risk I am running, because one day it might all be lost.

... *and its lust*

In a sense we have a dilemma when attempting to understand how love works. Certainly, there is something about attraction and appeal and what the other person 'does for us'. So we must accept that the first level of attraction (for men most always, for women not always) is visual, but then a little uneasiness catches us out - isn't that a bit superficial, shouldn't it be about loving the whole person?

"Of course", we want to say.

Nevertheless, now, even from that less carnal point of view, we still have to place the sexual impulse. We cannot make as if it has no part other than as a means of reproduction. Surely it cannot simply be so mechanistic, that part of our genetic makeup, albeit programmed with the promise of 'jouissance' (the French word itself conveniently combines the mechanical aspects of orgasm with the sense of 'joy'), which secures the continuance of the species.

Even as recreation and not just procreation, sex has always had an ambiguous significance in our sense of what relationship is about. This ambiguity arises not just through the commercial exploitation of sex on the one hand and its occasional disconnect from the motivation for long-term relationship on the other, but also from its increasing acceptance in our modern society as a vicarious pleasure-giving activity - no strings attached!

And all this now begins to sound as though we were relegating sex to 'merely' being a necessity in a committed partnership, an accessory in a romantic relationship, an occasional option in others. But no, not that either, for that is still to define a relationship in terms of the extent of its enacted lust. And love is something else.

... *always underneath, relation*

Perhaps there is another way to view this: relating is a process and sex is both the embodiment of that process and its enactment. Its significance is different for different couples, even within a committed romantic relationship, and so it is not to devalue it (nor hint at any moral stance) to say that the sexual impulse does not *per se* inform us about the essence of their mutual love. In similar vein if the nature, quality or frequency of sexual activity is an issue in the dysfunction of a relationship, that does not *per se* indicate any pre-emptive place for sex in defining what the relationship ought to consist of: in this case what is at issue is the partners' differences in expectation or need.

Partly our turmoil and our uncertainties come from that confusion caused by the language. We tend to think of love as if it had distinctly different versions and as if these were discreet and dissimilar, and yet despite this we call them all 'love'.

Even so, the issue is not one of changing names, but whether in essence platonic love, for example, is really any different from romantic love, romantic love any different from infatuation, and so on. Might it help our understanding of this aspect of our human experience (the one which produces the most, and the most extreme, highs and lows) to look on its 'versions' as simply alternative points on a continuum? Because losing a loved one, be they beloved or best friend, causes similar pain and grief. The nature of the loss we feel when love ends without our wishing it, is no different and can be just as intense, whether that loss is of a life-long friend or whether it is our partner. Sometimes it might even seem that we experience the loss of the life-long friend more acutely: there are many variables and it could be that what we have allowed to be known to another as a friend could be more deeply a part of our inner self and hemmed around with fewer no-go zones than what has been available to our partner. Whatever the nature of the loss, the same underlying emptiness.

... a process, a flow

In those moments, then, when the accustomed mechanical interaction between colleagues or casual friends, starts to contain something else, what is happening? The words might be the same, but the delivery and tone different, and the facial expressions, especially the eyes, would be changed. Our normal mechanical interactions, whether they be casual conversations about events or the weather, discussions on how something might be tackled, or even guidance to enable another to achieve something, are invariably self-centred - in this sense, that the end of the interaction will have completed something for us. Yes, in all cases, for us. We will have come full circle and arrived back at that point where we wait for the next interaction to start. (For those who are familiar with the Gestalt cycle of awareness and contact - withdrawal... sensation... awareness... mobilisation... action... contact... withdrawal - there will be similarities here.)

But when it is not quite like this, when what passes between us contains a feeling *for* and not just a feeling *about*, then what we have offered no longer completes something and we never quite come full circle. What is different is that we are wanting what we offer to 'do something for' the other, to make them feel good in some way, even if no more than by their sensing that we are wanting this for them. And for us the circle is not complete until we know that this has happened, for it will be complete only when we see a sign of confirmation... which indicates a mutuality.

... *through an offering and an accepting*

What is happening is that our wishing to give something to the person through our interaction holds us in suspense until we know (from the other's reaction) that what we are offering has been received and welcomed. The other's response may start its own cycle for them and then for us, but for now our circle has been completed. That wishing to give and willingness to receive has created something extra in the exchange. We have heard the music start to play.

There is an area called the Pla Mirenge in the foothills of the French Pyrenees, which over time had become overgrown with scrub and the gradual creeping of the ancient forests which are such a feature of the Ariège. A group was formed from local bodies, nature groups, landowners, municipalities, livestock producers, to clear large tracts of these hillsides, not with any commercial motive, but simply to allow the land to breathe again. With the undergrowth cleared, the grass grew back and then a few seasons later it was discovered that orchids, some of them only found in the Pyrenees and not seen for around forty years, had appeared and flowered.

Perhaps we have also discovered how to account for a love enduring, even when the music is not playing, for the wishing to give and the willingness to receive are a special kind of openness, like a wild orchid waiting for the next time to flower.

~ ~ ~

If we can see where lie the seeds of that emotion we call love in its unity of forms, we can better understand the ways in which it produces those feelings we associate with it, the fulfilment and the frustration, the jubilation and the dejection, in almost equal measure. For in looking at love as a process, we are less likely, when things go wrong, to project our pain as the 'fault' of another, or even castigate love itself for its injustices and its indifference. And so we open up for ourselves a path to recovery, for in projecting we disempower ourselves, but in understanding, we re-own the means to heal ourselves.

The trials of love are legion… from primary school through teenage years we experience the conflict between love's impulse and nature's inhibition... as parents we feel the tension between the mentor's principles and the nurturer's acceptance... and when that struggle is over, the challenges of love displaced, as the family home is forsaken... as young adults, with life starting 'for real', choices feel decisive, but always the shadow of rejection and the torment of jealousy... for any care-giver the torture of loving what they cannot keep safe... and at the end, the pain of caring as life slips away.

In all of these trials, the cycle of the lover's open gesture, willing a response, has been frozen, a hiatus has occurred, perhaps a rupture, perhaps simply a pause predicting transformation, but for a while the currency of love, the responding of the other with a willingness to receive, is in suspense. The suspension brings pain for the cycle is incomplete, like a wound which will not close and where the slightest touch will sting. Always there is present the striving to bring the parts together, but always there is fear lurking that the wound might not heal and the tissue not be perfectly re-formed.

In this way we can explain the outward signs of jealousy and yearning, misgiving and grief, that we connect with interrupted love...

> the rejected lover tries every means to regain contact - he texts, sends flowers and 'happens by' her house, and he's also tetchy, and demanding of others' attention to his story in its every nuance...

> the mother now alone in the house feels empty and distraught, at home she wanders restlessly and tidies the unused bedroom; with friends she talks ceaselessly about tiniest clips of news and success...

the husband caring for his wife with dementia exhausts himself with doing everything that can be done, for there were times, he knows, when he had not done that, and perhaps so long as now he is always attentive there will be glimpses for her of his unending love.

... *and love's wounds, life's imprint*

But not all love can be restored and every interruption leaves a mark. The minor interruption, the lover's tiff, heals well enough, though the bubble of euphoria has been pricked. But the parent whose child wanders into 'bad company' and self-abuses with alcohol or drugs faces an altogether greater challenge to believe the cycle can be resumed, and to keep themselves open and available, still wishing to give what is befitting, even when there is no willingness to receive.

And then, like Isabel Gramesón, and like everyone whose partner has left to go to war, to tolerate the hiatus of a love suspended can itself *become* the cycle, so that calm may come in the pauses each time the circle closes, for "this time, again, I've managed".

So, for each one who will be left, because no amount of care could ever have been enough, the cycle can resume through resignation... and now the circle closes because the part has been played to the end. CK Williams offers us a picture of the husband who will quietly play his part until the curtain falls: "... not any sort of secular saintliness - that would be belittling - it was just the next necessity he saw himself as being called to."[30]

---

[30] From 'Alzheimer's: The Husband' by CK Williams in 'New and Selected Poems' (Blood Axe Books, Newcastle upon Tyne, 1995)

Contemplation : on a life in touch

Life is a flow, from the moment we are born to the moment we die.

A *flow* is who we are and what we do... a person, yes, an object made up of component parts that manifest an image which we take for a character, making our stand in an identity needing to be acknowledged, having an idea about how things *should* be and what *ought* to be done, clinging to certainties about what we *know,* anxious to reinforce our preconceptions and disguise our frailties...

But a *flow* is also who we are *and* what we do... meeting hearing conversing sharing, involved with others always, so that the course which is our life is part of others' lives too, lives which would be different without us, as our life would be different without them...

I am only the one I am because they are the ones they are.

This grand flow of all living seems more like a tide.

Outside my control.

Like a flock of sheep, seen from a far-off mountain top, which swirl around, press in, peel off and scatter, then re-form… a flock, so many lives, slowly urging forward, movement onwards but not towards, finding a direction, but not craving a destination… needing and being needed in that community of humankind who are more like me than not like me, amongst whom I can be the one I am if I can only let them be the each they are… in touch with my flow and part of the tide's swell.

An Uncertain Passage

It is the second day of a retreat I often lead…

The teaching introduces meditation as a pathway for exploration, following way-marks of western psychotherapeutic discourse, and we arrive at a point where the key motifs resemble most closely a buddhist frame. There are many touching-points between buddhist and western psychology, but to look for causality to one or the other or even an antecedent status is not helpful: in articulating a conceptual framework in any tradition, we are only making tangible those facilities of the human mind which we all share and all use, even unknowingly, at some time.

To describe, though, is to uncover. It opens up the way for intention (for we cannot intend something for which we have no handle) and intention means agency, even if it be no more than to say "this shall be the direction of my next step".

We might describe them as 'states', these key motifs on

which we light - I describe them as the conditions of *impermanence, interdependence, insubstantiality*. Together they coalesce around the discovery that nothing exists, which brings to mind the parallel of the Buddha's dictum that "everything changes". And if profoundly felt, alongside the acceptance of the whole of our intellect, they can permeate our very being with a deep and resonating calm.

... *impermanence*

There is no such thing as stillness,
so there can be no such thing as permanence

It is almost facile to say that nothing is permanent, that everything changes, but yet in most aspects of our day to day living we act as if what we are in contact with, people places situations, will always be as we find them now and can be relied on to go on giving us the responses and results we have come to expect. In other words the future is predictable: this reinforces for us that we do not have to go through the inconvenience, perhaps distress, of reinventing how we work out our world. For what is more comforting than to be able to sail along in the certain knowledge that we have the measure of things and have an answer for whatever comes up, whether that is how to respond when repeatedly asked for a favour, or how to handle conflict at work? But in 'knowing' how something works and what to do, we have allowed our awareness to be dulled. In expecting no change, we give ourselves permission not to notice and not to listen. After all, why expend the effort to do that, when there is nothing new to learn and nothing to be gained? Stay in the comfort zone.

So what if we knew it differently? Need it be unsettling

if we weren't able to expect a thing to be as it was, weren't able to anticipate that someone will do as they have before? It depends on how we involve ourselves in the flow - the *how* of looking out at our world before the *what* that our senses bring to us. You could say our looking (and listening and feeling and tasting and smelling) needs to begin with a question mark - an inquisitive sense of "how am I feeling this?", before the blasé intellect kicks in and provides a label. Being enquiring allows a genuine meeting and the discovery of what really is, which can never contain a presumption of knowing what to expect, because it starts from an intention to find out.

Thus it can be with the way we see our world. Impermanence is predicated if we let living be synonymous with discovery. And vice versa: this practice of mindfulness is itself a component of our knowing of impermanence. But there is more to a deep acceptance of impermanence. In extending the notion to ourselves and allowing that we also are ever changing - on a physical level with the constant regeneration of our cells, on an immediate psychological level with an information flow to keep us functioning and on a longer term psychological level with a gradual updating of our attitudes - in recognising the impermanence of ourselves, we come up against a much more existential challenge. We must re-orientate. We must re-visit our understanding of how we know ourselves. All ideas of 'object' and 'fixed' and even 'character', depictions in which we see form, must be relinquished in favour of modulation and transcendence. For 'definition' substitute 'process': the deep acknowledgement of impermanence makes obsolete our recourse to "how we always are" and opens up the path of "how we might be". Re-phrasing (yet again) that much-used and endlessly re-worked quotation from George Bernard Shaw - "rather than grounding ourselves in how we are and finding comfort in the self-observation, we could open ourselves to how we might be, and then we can ask 'why not?'"[31] Further through the scene from which the original quote comes (see footnote), the serpent makes another disclosure which in our context we might take as a precept: "I fear certainty as you fear uncertainty... If I bind the future I bind my will. If I bind my will I strangle creation."

Our sense of who we are, then, must reside in knowing ourselves as a means of creating the present - for ourselves - and affecting others' presents, as they ours. For all that such a proposition might feel precarious, it is a base less vulnerable than any fixed notion of who or what we are, for in this way life and our idea of our 'self' is experienced as a process, always moving, always flowing, without fettered hopes or disillusioned optimism. Here at last is offered a sense of being at peace, a peace which regenerates and revitalises in each moment, a peace in which we need have no commitment to the person we were, a moment ago, yesterday, last month. But this is not an invitation to abdicate responsibility for our actions: we must be clear that the peace comes through the release from a commitment - to be as we always were, to do as we always did. With each step we take we have responsibility, and not just for what we do at that point, though certainly that. No, our responsibility extends to accepting the freedom of knowing that each next step heralds change, which will inevitably and always make a difference.

---

[31] George Bernard Shaw, "Back to Methusaleh, part 1, act 1", the serpent to Eve: "... I hear you say 'Why?' always 'Why?' You see things; and you say "Why?". But I dream things that never were; and I say 'Why not?'"

... *interdependence*

There is no such thing as isolation,
so there can be no such thing as independence

At any level of existence we care to consider it is a truism to say that everything happens because another thing happened before it. Whether we want to broaden that to declare a general law of cause and effect depends partly on our use of language. For many of us, 'cause' contains an implication of agency and ascribes a degree of intention or pre-ordination. That veers away from our sense of interdependence here. Here we need only observe that the cause has simply happened and the effect has happened in consequence. We can test this by trying out the opposite: if the cause had not happened then could the effect have been there? An effect is brought into existence by its cause and if we posit that an effect is inextricably linked to a specific space at a specific time, then each effect is unique, even if its cause may have given rise to multiple (and not necessarily similar) effects.

But interdependence is more than non-independence.

Recall Ubuntu: I can only be me if you are being you.

And it goes further even than the interpersonal implications of Ubuntu, because this starts within us before even we encounter others. What defines us, in the sense of showing the person we are, is what we do that is seen by others in the world, for there is no way of knowing a person for who they are other than by observing them through their actions. But to act we must have something to act on. Whether the action is a smile, or advice, or helping someone by repairing a fence, it cannot exist without a recipient. So before the person that is me can become real, by being seen through my actions, there must be the possibility of those actions being received. Likewise, for the possibility of receiving there must be an originator. At this fundamental level we are interdependent, for what we give must be able to be received and what we receive must have been able to be given.[32] For a therapist to use their qualities as a therapist, there must be a 'client'. For the therapist to develop their unique way of being with which to help the recovery of a particular client and so to make possible the unique achievement of their life, there must have been at least one particular and irreproducible meeting of that one client with that one therapist.

Dependence - or non-independence in our case - has negative connotations of need in the therapy field, where the watchword is empowerment. The therapist is committed to empowering the client so that they are able to make their own decisions in their own way about their own lives. This rests on the discourse of individualism which is embedded in the Western view of the world and each of our distinct (and distinctive) parts in it. Words like fulfilment, actualisation, consummation, all derive from the notion that there is virtue in finding one's own path and making one's own way. Dependency on the other hand is seen as introducing vulnerability, if not fragility, for what is at stake in the end is survival; survival, that is, of our identity as the person we know ourselves to be. Surrounded by a competitive world, with an in-built neediness to remain as we are because most alternatives are unsettling and may be unsafe, we might avoid the

---

[32] cf. the author's exploration of romantic love in "Stillness in Mind" (Changemakers Books 2014), pp. 80-81 'Love and its Confusions'.

vulnerability of dependency but only at the risk of introducing the anxiety of failure.

The proposition of interdependence runs counter to this received 'wisdom'. So do we panic too quickly in conflating dependency and need? Our unease arises from a fear of being left exposed - our safety-net taken away (by another's unilateral action) when it is too late for us to acquire the means to support ourselves - keeping control is, after all, the dominating trait in the human character. But complete security is a delusion and anyway the argument is circular, for if there were justification for the fear, then the belief in our own empowerment on which the philosophy rests could not exist. Likewise the anticipation of its loss.

We could say that such analysis is too cerebral for our context of sense and sensitivity, for here we are more concerned about the shift in sensibility which comes with the realisation that we are a part of what is living. Sometimes this might be felt as a relief that, despite a lingering unease at not having complete control of our own destiny, there is the comfort from something being shared. Sometimes it might be an uplifting sense of participation in something larger than the mundane intricacies of everyday life. Sometimes it envelops us, like a soft comfortable sofa, with a deep knowing that the world simply works this way.

... *insubstantiality*

There is nothing we can know except by presence -
the rest is our projection.

In the human psyche lies an arrogance which believes that whatever it sees, it knows. In reality the images which we receive and are reflected on our retina are no more than arrays of coloured light. What we 'see' is what our brain tells us we see; but our brain serves more than one master.[33] Images are matched by memory through approximation and selection, both of which are at the mercy of motive, temperament, opportunity, mood and other vicarious influences. In a few minutes, tomorrow, next week, next month, all these will be different and therefore what we would 'see' from identical arrays of coloured light would also be different. The substance of an image will have shown itself to be insubstantial. We may tell ourselves that we know what we see and that what we see is how things are, but yet the objects in our vision, which appear so solid, are really opaque, little more than happenstance, the product of chance appearance and our present consciousness. Christophe André[34] likens this phenomenon to a rainbow: whether we can see a rainbow - we could say, whether a rainbow exists - depends on where we are standing, where the sun is, there not being clouds, to the extent that, being in a different position, the rainbow might not be visible, might not exist for us. Likewise, of course, a rainbow which is visible to *us* may not *exist* for someone else. Reality is no more than a passing phenomenon without substance.

So, my friend with whom I had a difference of opinion yesterday, this morning walks past me with her head down and without greeting me in her usual way. I am hurt and a little panicked and a little guilty. Is my friend no

---

[33] Perhaps we would like to say that the brain *is* the master, but this is difficult to support when most often patterns of thinking and behaviour are shaped largely by conditioning.

[34] ch. 13, "Je Médite, jour après jour", L'iconoclaste, Paris, 2015.

longer my friend? because friends should be able to talk about things without falling out and I was willing to let bygones be bygones but not her it seems, so obviously I am a bigger person than she is, now that she is behaving in such a petty way! And then later that day I learn that her partner was rushed to hospital in the middle of the night.

The person that I believe I see may not be that person. That is not to say that what I am representing in the way I am representing it does not correspond with a physical being. It is not to deny physical existence. But what I have in mind as that person, that they are like this or like that, is simply in my mind and does not serve to let me discover their actuality, their complete actuality. Physical beings we can know because we can approach them and with all our senses 'touch' them, in this way knowing their presence. That much comes from them. But the mix of data which makes up their image in our head is simply that. And incomplete. Viewed from the perspective of yesterday or tomorrow or the next day they will be different.

~ ~ ~

Impermanence, interdependence and insubstantiality… not anything that we can be converted to, since they are terms for existential phenomena; not any aspect of faith, nor objects of belief, for that would suggest an act of trusting something of which it can only be said, "this simply is". They invite only our awareness.

~ ~ ~

In the Sufi tradition of Islam are many stories. This one tells of a king who has become very discontented…

> The king ruled many lands and whilst he did
> not want his subjects' lives to be miserable -
> because he liked to have other rulers look on

and be impressed by how he governed - nevertheless every last thing had to be carried out in the way that he decreed. Mostly things went well enough because his subjects were fairly settled - it was only occasionally that some revolutionary came to the fore and there started to be murmurings among the populace and then of course he had to deal with that, usually by 'disappearing' the troublesome person. But that was about the extent of any problems and the fact that the people seemed settled to his neighbouring rulers acted as a deterrent to would-be aggressors.

Try as he might the king could not work out the source of his discontent. He knew that he had everything set up perfectly. There was stability in the kingdom and if occasionally he had to make 'adjustments' in the interests of keeping everyone comfortable with their lives, well, that was just a minor inconvenience. He was absolute ruler; he knew exactly how things worked; no-one would tell him what to do because no-one else knew everything about everything as he did. So what was it he was feeling now? He wondered if it might be melancholy, though he couldn't see why, but he was more and more prone to outbursts of impatience and anger for no real reason at all.

In the end he called his wise men together and put the problem to them. He could not continue like this. It was necessary that he became happy again - for the good of his people of course. He would give them a week to shut themselves off, to talk and to contemplate and to find a solution and bring it to him. And just in case they needed an incentive to come up with something effective, if they didn't come back to him with a solution in the time, then he would 'disappear' them.

The wise men were perplexed at the king's demand. They instinctively felt that with everything working so well in the kingdom the solution to the king's difficulties would not be found in changing anything that was around him, rather it would be within the king himself that any change would have to come about. But how to convey this to him... and be around long enough to see him get better? They worked hard, all night towards the end, and on the appointed day they presented themselves in the court. Nervously they offered him what they had prepared for him - an intricately carved ring. And their spokesman stepped forward to explain their gift to the king:

"Your majesty, it might seem like a very little thing to give to a king who feels such great distress, but this ring is a symbol of everything that life contains for each of us.

Firstly it is a circle, the perfect geometric shape, which shows us that everything is required for completeness and that no one part is more important than another.

Secondly we can look at the ring and see it as the

form it is, a solid object; but we can also look at it and look through it and then it is like a moving window and what appears depends on how you are holding it.

And thirdly the ring has an inscription running around it, which has no ending."

At this the king looked at the ring and read the inscription and as he did so he began to feel his spirits lift.

It read: "THIS TOO SHALL PASS"

At different times it has been suggested that this story is based on the life of Ashoka, a very powerful Indian emperor of the third century BC, who ruled most of that sub-continent even as far as Afghanistan. He was reputed to be a bad-tempered and unkind man. He was despotic and ruthless in his use of his power. For eight years he waged wars with surrounding states to expand his empire, but at the end of one such war he was walking round the city his forces had just destroyed and was overcome with grief on seeing the extent of the destruction where there had previously been people leading their ordinary lives, the bustle of a city about its business, and now there was desolation and a haunting heavy hush. From that point on he ceased his warmongering, adopted buddhism and became a model ruler, establishing a fair code for his people carved on pillars for all to see, and setting up a model for the relationship between buddhism and the state which was viewed as an example to be emulated far and wide.

~ ~ ~

It is like we are being invited to give up what we always believed kept us safe.

"This too shall pass" can only mean I cannot know what will come next except that it will be different. Apart from death there is only one thing of which I can be certain... that I cannot be certain. Always, deep in our being, comes a quivering apprehension when we glimpse the reality that some aspect of our world tomorrow might not be the same as it is today.

There is a puzzling incongruity about this: that the only species on the planet with an innate drive to improve its condition and the intelligence to extend its reach (apparently without limit), the only species able to even conceive the possibility of overcoming all impediments and limitations, is also the species whose anxieties can impede its vision and shackle its momentum. Is this the innate pessimism of humankind? A primitive reflex in place before the realisation of intellectual superiority? Because it seems to fly in the face of the simplest empirical revelation - "This too shall pass", the good *and* the bad.

Or is this anxiety rooted in the perilous pretentiousness of the megalomaniac - perilous because of his own utter self-conviction?

In either case, the implication is that our best efforts to determine outcomes can never be more than just that - best efforts. So will we read this as a prognosis for depression or as realism that brings release and fortifies the soul?

There is another sense of this which hovers around our search for understanding, namely, the inevitable conclusion that there is nothing we can possess. We cannot own something as ephemeral as the passing of time, in the way that we believe we own a physical object. We scoop up water from the stream in cupped hands, but in a few moments it trickles away. We watch time passing in the changes and movements of the world around, in the slow dissipation of intense emotion, in the gradual easing of pain, in the chocolate slowly dissolving in our mouth, but there is nothing we can capture, no freeze-frame option is there, our only token is the reliquary of memory.

It might feel as if there is no solid ground anywhere. The human animal is so vested in its notion of ownership as being the proof - to whom? to itself, to other creatures, to the universe? - that s/he exists, that to question this premise threatens life itself and blocks any possibility of reappraisal. Like the child who stands fearfully and alone on the end of the diving board knowing that to take the plunge means only leaning forward and gravity will do the rest, so humankind fumbles with the anxiety-poisoned chalice of proprietorship while the currents of an interlaced creation flow past.

But for as long as we stand at the end of the board without entrusting ourselves to the flow, our survival is in jeopardy...

Stopping Dreaming

"At first I could not fathom the difference I was feeling. I could not even bring an image into my mind which was distinct enough to describe, to myself never mind to anyone else. It had something to do with light and then that seemed to transpose itself into lightness, and that struck me as pretty perverse in the circumstances. And then it seemed to be about vision, not just that it was clearer, though that was in it too, but it felt raw. Raw seems a bit brutal, and I suppose it was, but it wasn't painful.

"I remember wondering who had had the vision to design the waiting room for the scanners, with glass walls from ceiling to floor on three sides. For most of those waiting, life had closed in. But to look out is to connect and be connected. The atmosphere was tense and the room was silent apart from the calls for each next person, to go through for their scan or to be given their results. But you were still in the world, you could see the trees outside and the grass and cars and people going past. You were still connected.

"It was on the way home that it started to come to me. It was like ice which had cracked on a pond to make a myriad crazed shapes, but was starting to re-form into a solid sheet. I remembered the zen proverb - when you are unenlightened the snows of Mount Fuji are the snows of Mount Fuji; when you are seeking enlightenment the snows of Mount Fuji are no longer the snows of Mount Fuji; when you become enlightened the snows of Mount Fuji are the snows of Mount Fuji. Like scales being lifted from my eyes, I realised that the need to expect something from the future, to have a dream, if you like, had been taken away. Whether or not I was going to die ceased to form in my mind as a question. As if the future had been something I was constantly sketching, like a dream, because I had needed to do that, but now I had stopped sketching and at least for now I was still alive and time wasn't a question. I had stopped dreaming."

This was the description given by a client who came to see me shortly after a scan to assess the results of a cancer operation. What he seemed to be relating was an awakening to the world, in which nothing actually looked different and his experiencing of people and things in it was not changed in any material sense, but his relationship to it had changed. Cliché though it was, or so he thought, it seemed as if a veil had been lifted. The veil was the way he previously had felt the world as being "for him" and its reality as being his image of it. From that moment the world was just the world and he was just there. He felt it as a huge relief.

~ ~ ~

Awareness of the world as simply what it is and ourselves as simply alive in it, is an element, sometimes stated sometimes implied, in every spiritual practise which sees life's passage as a journey to a developed state. Whether along a path like buddhism through an internal enlightenment in the follower's mind or with a journey of faith, as in one of the monotheistic religions, towards a sense of 'oneness' with a deity, the moving out from the limitations of our construct of our place in a world which is also our construct, is its essence. Such a realisation can have a profound effect for an individual, as for my client, and it has vast potential for the society of humankind.

At first glance the proposition might seem nihilistic because it calls on no belief system and posits no moral code. But such an assessment would be superficial - like focusing on the trees of the mountain slopes and losing sight of the massif to which they cling. Or watching intently the single bee about its individual task without seeing the swarm which gives meaning to its existence. That is the partial view, but worse than that, it is the partial view taken to be the whole, for in being human-centric, it sees nothing outside its own field of vision.

A moral code is the mortar which holds together human society and to even countenance the notion that neither society nor its mortar is fundamental to our existence feels profoundly unsettling. Did Buber not say that to meet, to be in genuine relation, was to be human? And so we need society. And is society not the product of a collective will to be in relation in a constructive and supportive way? Buber, though, also saw the 'I-Thou' relation in the meeting between people as the reflection of humanity's (and each individual's) relation with the divine. The I-Thou of an individual person is brought into existence by the possibility of that relationship within an encompassing greater whole.

Shunryu Suzuki depicts an inner world and an outer world and our breathing as the connection... "When we inhale, the air comes into the inner world. When we exhale the air goes out to the outer world. The inner world is limitless and the outer world is also limitless. We say 'inner world' and 'outer world' but actually there is just one whole world... The air comes in and goes out like someone passing through a swinging door... When we become truly ourselves, we become the swinging door and in the purest sense we are independent of, and at the same time, dependent on, everything."[35]

In all the mystical branches of all the spiritual traditions of the world is the assertion of an essence of our being which is not our own construct and cannot be interpreted, can only be experienced. It is metaphysical, but it is also the tie which can hold us in our world... and it is the breath of our existence for as long as we honour the dependency of our independence. This primary tie is not a moral one but more like an existential plain which contains all evolving beings and their origin. The primal needs of existence - nourishment, grounding, breathing - come first and are processes of exchange. Hence our dependence. So far, so good. But then the impulse to transcend the primal and with indefatigable intellect claim a kind of independence. To assume that this capability confirms our freedom, though, is delusion, for that algorithm omits the critical constraint of resources and capacity. To some extent there can be a trade-off between our inventiveness and our level of consumption - resources can be 'increased' through technology and efficiency - but in the end it comes

---

[35] Shunryu Suzuki, 'Zen Mind, Beginner's Mind', Weatherhall, New York, 1970: part 1, 'Breathing'

down to the capacity of the planet, which is finite. Nature will always balance the equation, and the disappearance of humans will be no more than the extinction of another species...

Unless.

Unless, with deep awareness of our being as merely an element in the living of all living things - of the dependency of our independence, of being no less than, and no more than, a part of how the world exists... unless we can know ourselves as indissolubly bound up with the evolution of the planet. The evolution of all living things as a totality is a never-ending process - it is what we call Nature - and there can be no finality and no 'winner' because our body, the planet, is always what it is when it is.

It is a tragedy that the mystical traditions within christianity have shrunk to such minuscule proportions, and that other faiths - islam, hinduism and even buddhism - have become stridently politicised at their fringes. This is not to suggest that constructive political influence cannot be based in faith. But it is to lament that Sufi, Quaker, Hasid and many more alike do not form a weightier underlay for our different societies; societies which, for the most part, have been underpinned for millennia by faith-based cultures that they still acknowledge (at least when it suits) today. For many, a mysticism arising from a faith in a deity is a possibility which can be accepted if not understood, but it is the transcendence of the intellect not the focus on the deity which is the essence of mysticism, and it is this transcendence which is also the nature of a true awareness of our dependent independence. It is from this base, of the tie with our planet, that our salvation as a species must come.

If there is one human quality which we could name as the outcome for an individual of an awareness of themselves as indissolubly linked to the existence of the planet, it would be humility. And if the humility of individuals were manifest in the dealings and associations of humankind at family, society, national and global level, then relationships at the inter-personal level and policy outcomes at inter-governmental level would be dramatically transformed.

With humility come interpersonal qualities like kindliness, unselfishness, caring, empathy, generosity; and political qualities like honesty, goodwill, integrity, selflessness. Also with humility comes the acceptance that one person cannot know everything; that uncertainty has a place in our lives because not everything *can* be known; that 'right' and 'wrong' are relative in almost all circumstances. Starting from this point, all that we think we know is revealed as merely so many shadows of what actually is: with our certainties betrayed and our game-plan exposed, there is no alternative now to consensus and a pathway of collaboration laboriously hewn out across a windswept hillside. And if the consequence is progress slowed, a technology less eye-catching, achievements more modest, then so be it. For reflection and consolidation and patient exploration are investments for an enduring future, a future forged in the reality of the present, not wishfully glimpsed through the opaque curtains of a dream.

A Hazy Horizon

Right and wrong, good and bad, perfect and imperfect... to see something as 'this' and as 'not that' are symptomatic of the most limiting tendency of the human intellect. This insistence on duality permeates everywhere. Complex issues reduced to one-liners for conciseness and a good headline. Thinking subverted.

Mass-migration will undermine stable societies...

Free-thinking people believe in democracy...

Children aren't safe on the internet...

Wearing religious symbols is divisive...

'Indisputable' truths. For what? To feel secure?

Neat packing. Nothing messy. Like long divisions without remainders.

Of course it has its attractions, this clear-cut mindset. It saves thinking. The route is clear; the direction of travel as unflinching as the Appian Way. Who is not impressed by aerial photographs of Roman roads striking out across the submissive countryside straight as a die? Compare that to the Celtic pathways weaving and winding over bog and fen. But a coin has two faces and both are integral. The Roman Empire, which strode across Europe, Mesopotamia and North Africa, brooked no challenge, subjugated without mercy, imposed organisation… and brought peace; the Celts conquered no-one, fought amongst themselves, developed slowly and entwined life and art. The Romans left a legal system, the Celts their earthy mysticism. And both have been needed.

The duality-perspective may have a Western bias but the delinquency is in all our genes: the ready recourse to "I KNOW" and the straitjacket of certainty which that laces around us. When we think we see difference and use it to make a hard and fast distinction, we believe we know all that we need to know, and then that distinction becomes embedded. When we survey our domain, holding what we see in our world as 'object', we hard-wire the digital circuitry which only supports a state of one or zero and cannot allow the messy conjunction of one Thou with another.

The antithesis, and the antidote, is the open-ended inter-dependency broached with the realisation that being me depends on you being you. And, in the end, living with the uncertainty which means having to trust - in ourselves, in the possibility of human kindliness and humility… and perhaps, from that other age, in a quiet expectancy that love, even separated for half a lifetime by mountain and ocean, can live, waiting, like the orchid, for a reawakening.

From the still space of patient attention humanity's soul emerges, with its timeless yearning to be met by itself in another.

Letter to the reader : It matters what you do...

"Ring the bells that still can ring,
Forget your perfect offering,
There is a crack in everything,
That's how the light gets in."

(*Leonard Cohen from "Anthem"*)

Dear Reader,

I came late to much of the pithy wisdom which some rock music icons, such as Leonard Cohen, have offered. I wish I had picked up this one earlier. For me things were "ok" or "not ok" depending on whether they were perfectly formed according to my scheme of things. So something with a crack in it could not be ok. It wasn't worthy of its name, it didn't live up to its label... no, my label.

Then eventually I re-discovered Rumi - did the teacher appear or was the student ready? - and started to accept that being imperfect, if it contains all of what we are, can be perfect in its way. When I had first read Rumi's "The Indian Tree" my commitment to global fellowship was skin-deep and I was unprepared for its challenge, but a deepening and a maturing of this understanding is what this journey has been about. So if you have come with me this far, I hope you will take these last few steps...

"A learned man once said, for the sake of saying something - There is a tree in India: if you eat the fruit of that tree, you will never grow old and never die."

Thus it begins, The Indian Tree, and we go on a search for the tree in Rumi's poem, we interpret literally and look for an actual tree, then discover that "tree" was only a name that one person gave it and to others it appears differently, that in the end the name does not matter, is maybe even a hindrance, because it prevents us touching the reality. The reality is that there is a way past names, which are the source of all conflicts... "such unnecessary foolishness, because just beyond the arguing there's a long table of companionship, set and waiting for us to sit down."

We seek and we also witness. Seeking is hard-wired into our brains from the moment we observe difference and make a comparison, and it sets us on our relentless pursuit of the better, the bigger, the finer, the purer - living, as a process of myopic accomplishment that we mostly do not even recognise because our attention is committed to doing and achieving. But seeking is what we are always about, it is evidence of our existence and it is confirmed by the witnessing. And seeking and witnessing, both, are needed, for what is sought by one of us, even if it is not found, becomes part of another and the striving in the search is only manifest when it is witnessed. The hope and the witnessing co-create.

Le Clézio in his novel "Désert" paints a picture of passing Touareg travellers in the Sahara:

> "Who are you?"
> "Bou Sba. And you?"
> "Youemaïa"
> "Where are you travelling from?"
> "Aaïn Rag."
> "I am coming from the south. From d'Iguetti."

Both acknowledged. Nothing more. But, in the vast empty spaces of a desert which seems to assimilate anything that moves on its surface, life has happened. The process is beyond the meaning of the words and outside the physical encounter. Thus, witnessing might be mutual, and physical, as with Le Clézio's travellers, but still the connection between the happening and the witnessing is meta-physical, for the one does not owe anything to the other.

The chorus in the theatre of ancient Greece were witnesses to the action of the play. They served other purposes too - they filled in the plot for the audience and explained the significance of events; they served as foil, as confidant, as sounding board for the leading characters - but principally they witnessed. Their presence turned tv drama into an epic; the parochial struggle of individuals into another footfall along humanity's highroad. If the confrontations between the heroes and the gods in Greek tragedies are seen as the intra-psychic turmoil of the human mind, product and incarnation of divine retribution, then the chorus is the listener who validates with an empathic ear.

Witnessing. The listener just listening. Not advising. Powerless to intervene.

To what end?

Why does an infant, newly mastered crawling, take off across the floor and just before it goes out of sight look round? Instinct for safeguarding risk? Perhaps, but also maybe to make a mark - "You've seen me, haven't you?"

In the adult, though, there is more involved. To ensure *we* are seen - noticed - is often self-serving. But to know that what we *do* has been seen can be more than this, for it can prompt reflection and even emulation in others. In the interest of the common good? Not of necessity, but we might hope, even intend, so. And then a link is created, not exactly a relationship in the sense of a meeting, more ephemeral than that, but a link in the chain of human interaction, the sense in which the past is always contained in the present. This is the nature of humanity's pathway, a path which is marked out and trodden and followed all at the same time.

History is this linkage, though the telling of it is always incomplete because nothing happens out of context and the context can never be completely known, containing, as it does, not just physical events, but the emotions and intentions of the players. Emotions and intentions. These cannot be read and told like the events themselves - they are history's blindspot - yet they contain the only key to the understanding of meaning. This brings us face to face with the inevitable realisation that the link, which is no more than the joining of 'before' to 'after', can never be deciphered looking back, the perspective of all historical accounts, because experiencing and witnessing have to be one.

So what is in this responsibility, for responsibility it is, of witnessing? No less than to be open and, being open, to notice and, noticing, to create space and weight and existence within ourselves for what is alongside but separate. Of itself the responsibility is not one to act, though there might be that impulse, but rather to broaden our reach. In doing no more than creating an existence for the other within our existence we have pre-empted a void.

In a station siding in full view of every train that stops at Le Vernet d'Ariège in southern France stands a cattle wagon covered with pictures of faces - the village had housed a transit camp for Jews during the second world war.

In many contexts and in many places we preserve images and memorials of those who have lived and are no longer known: that metaphysical connection - "I would have wanted you to know that I see you" - the now present past in the passing present.

But can there not be more? *Should* there not be more? A chain is not just the links, it is the process of linking as well. Can I witness and allow myself not to be affected? Even the chorus in ancient Greek tragedies could own to an emotional response at times. Surely even we, travellers along humanity's pathway, must allow ourselves to be stirred. And if I witness, why *would* I not act? Just witnessing cannot be enough. Yet the scope of one individual's intervention seems so minuscule. True, it is granted to very few to play a lead-role on the grand stage, but that is to confuse the lustre for the colour, to mistake the outcrop for the mountain.

Separate the micro and the macro. Disassemble the public edifice. Look past the sheen of presentation. In no realm of human activity can there be lauded achievement without humbler support. In the prosecution of public works, charisma is a veil which masks the true centre of influence, for a leader does not lead in isolation. That saying from buddhism which tells us that "when the student is ready, the teacher will appear"... for "teacher" read "leader"... ponder on this for a few moments and a question arises - does the presence of the teacher/leader beget the student/

follower or is it the other way around? Even, do they co-create as inter-dependent? For if so, then the true centre of influence, in learning, in building a fair society, in resolving conflict, in achieving peace, is in the togetherness of spirit and the being in communication - the process, that is, and not any individual. And to project the responsibility onto others, even from a stance of humbleness, is to opt out.

The solution to all human challenges begins not from macro-concepts, but in micro-actions. Actions prompt exchange. Exchange requires dialogue. Dialogue - true dialogue - is a meeting. True meeting means surrender - surrender of certainty, surrender of assumptions, surrender of self-centredness... and an openness to being a part of *all* our futures. Humility. Inter-dependency.

The micro at its most fundamental level is within us. It is the challenge that is the primordial metaphysical conflict for humankind, the double-bind of humanity, the two-edged sword of our consciousness. Resolution would be transcendental, for ever since the human being could turn inwards and look on itself, see itself and distinguish itself from others, walk out across the plain of multi-dimensional comparison, comparisons in space and time, in identity and possibility, it knew the tension between the drive to be better - better than before, better than others - and the surrender of its self-obsession, that tension which blocks the way to a true meeting. Our cleverness and its technology has brought us from the discovery of fire to the exploration of planets, but it has also broken the perfect machine of Nature... for ever, or for a while? From where we are now, the rendezvous of human kind with its apocalyptic destiny of an over-heated, over-populated planet (and all the contingent problems) can only be delayed by the engagement of every individual at every level in their every action on every day - because that is their part to play, and it matters what they do. Then just perhaps the delay may be able to be made permanent.

In the sphere of the practical there are many projects and much goodwill, on a plain removed from the politicking and the posturing. The ingenuity of humankind can stretch resources, creating an illusion of inexhaustibility, but still the infernal mechanism grinds on as the prison door slowly closes. Rays of light burst through the crack - *global population will peak at 10 billion* - but are then extinguished - *and the ageing demographic will not be able to sustain its needs.* Global warming could be halted, but by then an increasing shortage of fresh water and a shrinkage in habitable land will have brought mass migration and devastating conflict. And still we delude ourselves that the answer will come from macro projects - because escapism is also in our nature, escapism into the good life, eco-friendly self-sufficiency, escapism in a creed of unwavering obedience, escapism into a Candide-like fantasy of "everything for the best in the best of all possible worlds". Yes, there are many living-strategies that are appropriate for addressing *individual* predicament, but they cannot be extrapolated to the global, for no project can ever command universal adherence because of the diversity of human perception and self-interest. In some way all these and many more are macro solutions, strategies 'handed down' to us, which we each test against our own pre-conceived standards, sometimes adopt, more often reject... and so none have the potential to shift a whole population to the tipping-point - the point at which micro *becomes* macro, rather than macro seeking to *work* the micro.

In the first chapter I suggested that our species "could do ill and could do well, could wound itself and could restore itself, but could never change its fundamental nature", and also that "it would always be searching for the healing pathway, the pathway to a kind of freedom". The next step on *that* pathway is no further than the next person we meet, be that in looking across the room or walking down the street, for in the nature of each contact we make is the micro process of meeting, which can *become* macro, and carry us all to the tipping-point.

Too often the person we think we see is the person we 'need' to see in order to satisfy our own biased and partial view of reality - we might say the person we see is a reflection of ourselves - so that with megalomaniac certainty we can carve out the world as if all that is required is *our* force alone. But yet our force, inadequate as it will always be, can be augmented and transformed by those others if we allow them to truly be who *they* are, with all *their* might. Then, finally, unconstrained by myopic defensiveness, the energy of the meeting will reach beyond, to the next meetings and the next, its curve becoming exponential, with the power to entrap humanity in benevolence, as it carves out the path which leads to the tipping-point.

Every place every time every meeting,
it matters what you do.

Simon Cole

About the author...

Simon Cole BA(Econ) MA(Counselling) MBACP (Snr Acc) has been a practising counsellor and therapist for over 30 years. After working for several years with the Samaritans, he qualified as a counsellor at Newcastle University and gained a Masters degree with distinction from Ripon & York St John (then affiliated to Leeds University), later training also with Joseph Zinker.

Author of articles for counselling journals in the UK and Australia, he worked for many years within NHS primary and secondary care, whilst leading the counsellor training programmes at advanced level at Carlisle College.

Since 2007 he has run a residential retreat centre with his wife in south-west France. There the emphasis is on a therapy which picks up the natural rhythm of the surrounding hills and mountains and works with self-discovery through mindfulness and meditation, combining this with creative counselling, music, poetry, writing and walking. Mindfulness and meditation have for many years been a vital part of his life and they have formed an increasingly significant part of his therapeutic approach. From this has come the formalising of the Clear Space Meditation Path, inspired by the move to France and the ambience of *Le Sentier Tranquille* retreat centre.

web: www.life-counselling.co.uk
email: simoncole@btinternet.com

Printed in Great Britain
by Amazon

21190737R00089